EMBRACING Aging

Discovering Fulfillment through
Coping with Life's Changes

EMBRACING Aging

Ruth Garrett, PhD

Providence House Publishers

PROVIDENCE PUBLISHING CORPORATION
FRANKLIN, TENNESSEE

Funding for this book was provided through a grant from Health Resources and Services Administration (HRSA).

Printed in the United States of America

13   12   11   10   09   1   2   3   4   5

Library of Congress Control Number: 2009938572

ISBN: 978-1-57736-425-2

Cover and page design by LeAnna Massingille

PROVIDENCE HOUSE PUBLISHERS
238 Seaboard Lane • Franklin, Tennessee 37067
www.providencehouse.com
800-321-5692

To my mother, Amy Barnett Manning McCall, who instilled in me the character traits that have helped me most throughout life: valuing and accepting all people, regardless of color, educational level, or religion.

To my two children, Amy Gregory Weeks, MD and David Kelly Gregory, PhD, so close to my heart, who have responsibly developed their lifestyles and professions, loved and accepted my strengths and weaknesses, and continue to dedicate their lives to their families.

To my brothers and sisters who have lovingly tolerated my strong democratic, liberal, political, and social concerns. As was taught by our mother, they continue to accept the challenge of searching for truth, while maintaining a dialogue with those whom they love.

— CONTENTS —

Preface ix

Acknowledgments xvii

One: Pondering the Meaning of Later Life 3

Two: Sinking 17

Three: Surfing and Making Lemonade 31

Four: Midlife in Perspective—Edit or Regret It! 43

Five: The Copernican Switch 69

Six: The Power of Perception—Attitudes Matter 79

Seven: Narcissistic Injury and Loss 103

Eight: Denial 135

Nine: Coping—The Key to Adjustment in Later Life 153

Ten: Successful Aging in Retirement—Retirement

      Precedes Aging; Aging Precedes Death 179

Eleven: From Fashion to Passion 199

Works Cited 225

About the Author 233

— PREFACE —

While employed as a teacher with the University of Maryland European Division in Germany, I resolved to improve my language skills, as well as my knowledge about German culture. After taking all Goethe-Institut courses that my husband's civilian employer would reimburse, I challenged the entrance test with three hundred forty other foreigners at the Ludwig-Maximilians-Universität (also called the University of Munich). Eureka! I was one of forty students who passed!

As a master's level student of German studies, I audited a seminar that was described as "women's issues." This exposure to global changing demographics focused on the challenges of older women and introduced me to the subject of gerontology (GRN). The retirement age in Germany had just been lowered, which seemed as illogical as my professor who harped on the miseries of growing older. She was the same age as I and of many of my fellow students. We agreed that, at least until the present, aging had not been a negative experience. Neither could we comprehend the reasoning behind the German government's move to lower their retirement age just as the United States of America was raising its own. Differences in the politics of nations strengthened my interest in aging and the issues that affect older adults. I immediately changed direction of study from linguistics to aging issues, moved up to the doctoral level (after interviews with academic advisors), and spent the next four years in an academic foreign university environment that changed my life. I was required to speak German like a native (except with an accent) and was privileged to interview many older Germans about their experiences in living through the two World Wars. Amazed at the resilience of older German women, I listened intently to how they had managed to cope with many changes as they fled their enemies. I was astonished at their enthusiasm, adaptability, and general well-being. My admiration of their survival skills strengthened my belief that the aging process could be better than what was taught at their university! I had no premonition at the time of how intensely I would personally and professionally become dedicated to aging issues.

Following a decade of life in the German culture, it was quite coincidental that my first professional involvement in aging issues occurred. We returned to Palo Alto, California, home office of my husband's employer. Daily researching aging studies at the Stanford University Library, I visited the Santa

Clara County Board of Education to enroll for substitute language teaching, mostly to maintain my German ability. I mistakenly entered the wrong door and applied, only to learn the next day that fate had sent me to the Adult Education Office. I was called by the director the next day and was offered an interview to discuss the development of aging programs. Located in an environment where older adults were above average in socioeconomic status, the exposure to resourceful, vital older adults set in motion my understanding of what is possible for the latter years of life. The comparison of two older female populations—the German Traeumer Frauen (WWII widows who, with their bare hands, cleared the streets of rubble and laid the groundwork to rebuild their cities) and the more privileged older women of Palo Alto was striking. The resourcefulness shown by Munich survivors appeared to result from the development of coping skills during difficult times. They were highly motivated survivors. The older women of Palo Alto, privileged to live in an extremely desirable environment of sunshine and cultural enrichment, were also resourceful, but needed stimulation, self-confidence, and leadership to trigger revitalization and productivity. A fortunate housing location and a little luck had led me to my flock! My challenge was to apply to aging Americans what I had learned from the exceptional agers of Munich. I had seen, first-hand, alternatives to the practices of disengagement and to the frustrations of unlimited leisure time that I had observed in many American communities.

Compensation and adaptation, or the idea that seniors must learn new ways of navigating their daily lives in order to adjust for possible physical and mental changes, is challenging. Restored purpose comes not only from a life review, but also from a life preview that offers exciting possibilities for healthy aging, vibrant wellness, and an expectation of meaningful longevity. My vision invites people to retire *to* something instead of *from* something; to a new vision of retirement that creates hope and expectation.

Challenges and experiences are catalysts for behavioral change. Communities can galvanize groups of people around the concept of aging well, as expressed through several core components of healthy living: social relationships, physical and mental well-being, nutrition and diet, arts and creativity, financial planning, and cognitive/intellectual vitality—especially the latter.

The establishment of non-profit, grassroots coalitions for building community with small groups of seniors who wish to grow old where they grew up is our challenge. Small-group models can create an educational, social environment where seniors learn new habits and information to promote total wellness, while they remain active and involved at home and in their immediate community. Sharing resources and information to solve common problems such as transportation, health care, and logistics of daily life can help create communities in areas where extended family does not exist. In extended neighborhoods, older adults can experience healthy, vibrant lifestyles in their communities without being institutionalized and without being financially drained from the offers of expensive, helplessness-inducing programs and services. With a vision of the future and concern for those whom we leave behind, mobilization of resources for a higher quality of life can be accomplished. We must create something new because the old solutions are not appropriate for today's challenges. As Harold Waldwin Percival (1946) said, every destiny begins with a notion. It is not our fate that our creativity declines as our bodies change. The greatest challenge for the twenty-first century is for creative thinkers to develop programs using the abilities and wisdom of older people that will release their full potential and harness the energy of millions of aging individuals. Without accepting a mortgage on their future, older adults can meet their needs by building community. The task requires that we challenge ourselves to enhance our mental abilities, to realize the relationships of cognitive, physical, and emotional qualities, and to solve challenges throughout one's entire life (Cohen 1977). Learning must become a way of life. We are entering a stage of full development in which lifelong creative abilities are expressed, and in which lifelong learning and development should be institutionalized by society (Moody 1987).

This publication investigates specific aging conditions that contribute to a higher quality of life in the latter decades. Adults age fifty and older are much healthier than their predecessors, and they have the potential to live independently much longer. A longer life is meaningless without preparation for one of the most significant developments of our times: the increase in life expectancy.

* * * *

On a blistering hot summer day in 1992, I walked to my Savannah, Georgia mailbox and removed its overfilled contents. A thin, blue airmail envelope bearing a Vienna, Austria postmark fell to the hot pavement. A closer look at the envelope revealed a return address that made my heart skip a beat. I ripped open the envelope: there was a letter from Eleanor (Elly) Frankl, second wife of Dr. Viktor Frankl. It was in response to the letter I had sent this world-famous Austrian psychiatrist. I had written to thank him for his heart-felt, scholarly documentation of his personal experiences in Nazi concentration camps, his ingenious methods of coping during this hellish incarceration, and his development of a school of psychotherapy, namely logotherapy. I had read several of his books, and had reread *The Will to Meaning* several times. I wanted him to know how he had inspired me and the content of my doctoral dissertation about aging (in German) at the University of Munich, a copy of which I had included with the letter. I had not expected any acknowledgement or response from him.

This letter from his wife explains that, because of partial blindness, her husband could no longer read. Accordingly, she had read portions of my book to him, and she noted that he had listened with "much attention and interest."

A copy of this book will be forwarded to Frau Frankl to show my gratitude for her response, and to pledge my dedication toward spreading the philosophy and wisdom of her late husband. Prophetically, after returning to America in 1983, I had actually heard Dr. and Frau Frankl at an American Society on Aging (ASA) Convention in Washington, D. C. I still remember Dr. Frankl introducing his wife to the ASA audience, with beautiful praise, and with the comment that he would never travel anywhere without her. Below is the letter I received from Eleanor Frankl.

Viktor E. Frankl, M. D., Ph. D.
1 Mariannengasse
Vienna, Austria 1090
Telephone 42 64 36

30. Jun 1992

Sehr verehrte Frau Dr. Garrett,

da mein Mann wegen seiner partiellen Erblindung nicht mehr selber lesen kann und wir täglich mit 1 bis 2 Dutzend Poststücken konfrontiert sind, darunter Bücher und Manuskripte, war es nur möglich, daß ich ihm Teile aus Ihrem Buch vorlas.

Ich kann Ihnen nur versichern, daß er mit größtem Interesse und ebenso großer Aufmerksamkeit zugehört hat!

Indem ich Ihnen seinen Dank für die Einsendung Ihres Buches ausspreche, verbleibe ich mit allen guten Wünschen von uns beiden

(Eleonore Frankl)

— ACKNOWLEDGMENTS —

Several examples of successful aging have influenced my professional involvement in aging issues, as well as my own personal aging. First, there was an agile, intelligent, retired eighty-five-year-old Bavarian music teacher, Herr Simon Decker, who was the village patriarch of Tuntenhausen, Germany. Second, my eighty-seven-year-old father who quietly passed away while I was writing my dissertation. Both men instilled in me the belief that I was capable of accomplishing whatever I wanted to do. Both were examples of how one can grow old solemnly and productively. Both continued to enhance their knowledge, to maintain family relationships, and to strengthen social responsibility. Although suffering from chronic diseases, both exhibited healthy attitudes and showed that it is possible to integrate the often problematic, aging-specific problems into their lives while increasing emotional and social strength, and slowing down the physical process.

My mother, Amy, taught me the importance of the quality of human relationships. She valued people—all people.

Acknowledgments

Though her burdens were heavy and contributed to her chronic illness, she instilled in those around her the importance of empowerment through love and acceptance of each other. We were never allowed to criticize another family member, whether it was a new in-law or a combative brother. "Look for the good because there is a good side of every human—focus on that and that will strengthen you." She taught us the value of reaching out to others. During World War II, when the army occupied our farms to train soldiers for duties in Europe, she would invite all those men near our home to come after supper and sing to her accompaniment at the piano. Many fell asleep from their demanding duties during the day and would sleep on the floor of our home until they heard the bugle call the next morning. My mother would naively explain that some French mother would be doing the same for our brother, drafted into the U.S. Air Force.

And, I thank my academic role models, Professor Doctor Bruno Hamann, who monitored my progress as a doctoral student, generously shared his expertise, his family, and his time with me, and who continues to write in several languages as a retired professor emeritus in Heidelberg. Dr. Walter Bortz' book, *We Live Too Short and Die Too Long: How to Achieve and Enjoy Your Natural 100-Year-Plus Life Span,* has been my personal guide for how we should live to enjoy a long and productive life. His other books, *Dare to be 100, Living Longer for Dummies, Diabetes Danger: What 200 Million Americans at Risk Need to Know*, and his 2009 publication, *Next Medicine: The Coming Revolution that Will Change American Health*, should be required reading for every professional and para-professional working with elderly adults, as well as for the adults themselves. I also thank Dr. Viktor Frankl and wife, Eleanor. Dr. Frankl is a Viennese psychiatrist and author of *The Will to Meaning* and numerous other books and articles. He was the most influential thinker I have ever read and met.

Thanks to my husband, Gary, who encouraged and supported me graciously in the necessary technical growth to accomplish this product, and who assumed many of the management tasks of daily life. Also, to my small fanclub of friends, namely Carol Galvez-Gutierrez and Peter Miller whose ongoing logistical support helped me to complete this project, and to Dagmar Dolatschko, for translation advice and assistance. And, finally to my two children, Amy Gregory Weeks, MD and David K. Gregory, PhD, who continued their development throughout my personal and professional adjustments, and who remain a stable and joyful influence.

EMBRACING Aging

one

PONDERING THE MEANING
OF LATER LIFE

"If life comes to an end while still incomplete, if everything comes to an end while still incomplete, what is the sense in it all?"

The Greek philosopher Empedocles

W hile standing in the Marienplatz several years ago, I was stopped suddenly by the resounding words of the late Pope John Paul II blasting throughout Munich's Central Square from a microphone: "Aging should be the crown of life; it should bring in the harvest—the harvest of all that we have learned, experienced, accomplished. Like the last movement of a great symphony, the important themes of life should come together in one triumphant movement." Who better than a seventy-year-old man, whom I highly respected, could confirm what I believe about aging? However, as I stood in that misty snowfall and reminisced, I knew that very few elderly experience the crown of life portrayed by the pope.

With tears streaming down my cheeks, I recalled experiences of my childhood. As I rode horseback by the "county house" near my home in Carthage, Tennessee, I could hear elderly individuals calling for help, sobbing loudly, demanding attention—attention that the limited staff could not or would not provide. Those homes, created for the elderly in the 1930s, became the nursing homes of today. Back then they were called "old age" homes or, sometimes, county houses. Not for profit, staff in these homes did not know the demands of today's nursing homes.

Patients didn't live long then, and sophisticated technology and government demands were relatively unknown. Unfortunately, then as now, many who entered the nursing home care industry had little or no professional knowledge and/or expertise with which to deal with vulnerable older persons. Rather than responding to the needs of the elderly with passion, the long-term care industry became a real-estate opportunity. Lack of quality care was the price that old folks paid (Goldberg 1996).

Gorgias von Leontine, Socrates' teacher, was one hundred seven years old when he was asked why he wanted to live so long. He responded: *"Nihil habeo, quod accusem senectutem"* (Cicero 1979, 22). Did the pope and Leontine really "have no reason to reproach old age," or was it Herman Hesse who wrote *Der Dichter* (The Poet) who was the lonely realist?

Hesse's poem describes the challenges of aging that both society and individuals impose on older people—that older adults are not allowed to yearn for a future, but only to wither and to die. It is not so much the physical difficulties, but rather the images from society that make old folks aware that they are growing old, alienating them from society, and consequently from themselves. On the one hand, society pictures aging as an achievement; on the other hand, society's reflections portray a picture of misfortune. This paradox was documented clearly by Ronald Blythe:

> *Aging, like illness and death, reveals the most fundamental conflict of the human condition: the tension between infinite ambitions, dreams, and desires on the one hand, and vulnerable, decaying physical existence on the other hand. This paradox cannot be eradicated by the wonders of modern medicine or by positive attitudes toward growing old.* (1979)

5

Nor can positive attitudes eradicate culturally-embedded experiences. For example, on another bone-chilling morning in Munich as I left classes from the University of Munich, a Turkish student walking alongside me asked, rather abruptly, "Why do you work so hard to master German? A woman your age in my country would already be dead!" In my early forties then, and planning to dare to be one hundred, I was shocked by his question, but maintained my international decorum. I explained to him that to remain alert the brain must continue to be used, and that we must challenge the brain at every age, but especially as we get older.

Three decades later, I continue to ponder why aging is so different in various cultures and why we age so differently even within our own culture. Pondering about life has always been part of the aging process. Many centuries ago, the Greeks also asked questions about the meaning of late life.

So then, how does an older person summon the fortitude to face the paradox of aging? My hearing loss, my rotator cuff pains, my arthritic knee, and my dental problems cause me to question my sometimes cock-eyed optimism about the future. If there is a meaning to life, how can one ever really know this meaning, and how can one remain positive when facing the changes of late life—physical, mental, social, or financial?

Canadian psychologist Gary Reker defined meaning as "the cognizance of order, coherence, and purpose in one's existence, the pursuit and attainment of worthwhile goals, and an accompanying sense of fulfillment." Reker developed the LAP (life attitude profile) test to help us examine our meaning in life. The LAP involves purpose, direction, coherence, control, goal seeking, personal meaning, death acceptance, and lack of an existential vacuum (Reker and Chamberlain 2000, 41).

Viktor Frankl, the Austrian psychiatrist and founder of logotherapy (therapy with meaning) who was incarcerated by the Nazis in World War II, said "The need to discover the meaning of things is impossible to eradicate from the human heart" (Tournier 1978, 189). He described the existential vacuum as the lack of meaning in life, inner void, or a desperate feeling of emptiness (Frankl 1967). He advised that man needs an anchoring place in life and that meaning is the rope to that anchoring place. Many find an anchoring place in worship of God. Others, such as Freud, proposed that sex was the driving force in man. Adler promoted the will to power as the motivating force and anchor in our lives. Frankl believed that only meaning gives us security, purpose, happiness, and sanity. However, he advised that meaning has to be discovered by each of us individually—it is a process of discovery (Frankl 1967).

Increasing one's responsibility can lead to the discovery of meaning. "If architects want to strengthen a decrepit arch, they increase the load which is laid upon it, for thereby the parts are joined more firmly together," Frankl declared (1984, 127). He advised his patients to take time and their use of time very seriously; we must take care of the minutes and not worry about the hours. We must be fully aware of our responsibilities—for the new gift of life that many of us enjoy, way past what used to be called old age. Life is not just something, but an opportunity for something and aging well means accepting the gift of life with thankfulness for the past and responsibility for the present and the future. We are responsible for actualizing the potential meaning of our lives, and the older we grow, the more responsible we should be. The realization that we must face death and the realization that we have not lived fully, correctly, and seriously—or perhaps that we may not really have lived at all, and that the offer of life will soon be over—can lead to despair in later life (Frankl 1984). However, it is never too late to begin to use time wisely.

I was surprised when I heard Jimmy Carter report that the average senior citizen spends forty hours a week watching television. Carter's life has not allowed much time for television. He has continued to contribute through his woodworking abilities and through ongoing community improvements such as Habitat for Humanity. Television, used correctly, has benefits for older adults, but not to the exclusion of continuous personal growth, staying involved with family and community, and maintaining relationships as we lose others. Excessive and passive television viewing can increase our risk for dementia.

I was alarmed when I read that one of every five older adults displays problem-gambling behaviors when they enter a casino. Older adults with minor physical disabilities may be drawn to the casino atmosphere, since gambling is a physically passive activity that provides an exciting adrenaline boost. Older adults with more choices for social interaction become less dependent on gambling as their only outlet. Gambling may fill a social void in their lives (Zaranek and Lichtenberg 2008).

Existentialism, proposed by Danish philosopher Søren Kierkegaard, focuses on living outside ourselves. It could be interpreted as "exiting" (leaving or forgetting) the focus on ourselves—our loneliness, our aches and pains, our "pale images of whom the future, the fulfillment of the world has no further need." There is a great need for each of us to reach out and live every day as if it were our last opportunity to add meaning to our life and to the life of another person. Our unending efforts to find meaning at the personal level, in our private lives and pursuits—rather than in recognizing an identity larger than ourselves—can lead to a meaningless existence. Without an understanding of life, of where we are and where we came from, we have no sense of past, present, or future (Frankl 1984).

When I was around forty years of age, I noticed that many of my friends were experiencing the empty nest syndrome. I had always heard that life begins when the children leave home and the dog dies. For many, life was beginning. Their children were thriving, and for many friends, the dog had left with the kids. A review of conversations with friends at midlife left me puzzled. One couple was planning their fourteenth cruise. Because I felt I must be missing something I awarded my husband, upon completion of his master's degree at age forty-five, with a cruise through the Caribbean. That was great—a wonderful diversion. Returning home, and to our jobs, we had been "re-created." Recreation had served its purpose—we went back to work with renewed energy and dedication. But, still puzzled by discussions with friends and their pursuit of pleasure, I was alarmed by their tenacious attempts to experience every kind of diversion. Troubling thoughts about how this could continue for thirty or more years increased my obsession with trying to understand what happens at midlife and beyond.

I was involved in conversations with my friends about liposuction, anti-aging medicine, life extension, surgical intervention, chemicals, dyes, cosmetics, braces, padding, costumes, and endless lists of other means of masking the aging process. I listened respectfully but silently questioned: Does looking younger have anything to do with being biologically younger? Does it extend life? Does looking younger add meaning to life? Does it strengthen the heart? Does it prevent or predict cancer? I remembered hearing a doctor advise that these interventions have no validity for human life extension. The paradox puzzled me. The market for cosmetic procedures is booming—a 15 billion dollar business! We are obsessed with the perfect image. For many, overhaul of appearance takes priority at midlife. We admire the beautiful and personally hunger for transformation (Kuczynski 2006). The loss of meaning is often accompanied by the panic feelings of older people that they must take their youth with them into old age. The graying of the population would more accurately be called the "tinting" of the population. Americans fifty-five and older spend 40 percent more than the national average on personal care and health products. This includes 37 percent of all facials, weight-loss treatments, and health spa memberships (Dychtwald and Flower 1989).

The current success of skin whiteners that claim to remove age spots is estimated at 90 billion dollars. The market for similar anti-aging products is booming. What lotions and potions can't do, the knife or laser might. Although the number of facelifts has decreased, cosmetic surgery is one of the fastest growing medical specialties. Chemical peels have increased by 67 percent, eye lifts by 31 percent, mastoplexies (breast lifts) by 26 percent, and abdominoplastics by 37 percent! Many have their wrinkles injected every six to twelve months with animal collagen, which helps to plump them up and smooth them out. Botox is the latest rage. Also, joining this race to look young is micro lip injection, in which fat cells are suctioned out of one part of the body and injected into a laugh line or a forehead crease. The number of men seeking cosmetic corrections has enhanced this very big business. Surgical techniques of hair transplants are multiplying—some costing as much as twenty thousand dollars (Dychtwald and Flower 1989). Is this the result of an existential vacuum—a lack of meaning?

The plight of the elderly in a narcissistic society is critical because they have so little on which to fall back or on which to look forward. The narcissist has so few inner resources that he looks to others to validate his sense of self. Unable to achieve satisfying sublimations in the form of love or work, he finds that he has little to sustain him when youth passes by (Lesnoff-Caravaglia 1985). In a sample of elderly people in San Francisco, sources of high morale and low morale were identified. Entertainment and diversions topped the list of high morale factors. Is it not absurd to even suggest that people fulfill their lives by exchanging what they have learned to do in their previous life for recreational pursuits or entertainment? Trivialization of life contributes to decline and to the withdrawal from society of millions who, instead of wearing out, rust out. There is an increasing need for meaningful activity if persons are to survive.

The denial of aging is one cause of low motivation in the elderly. To accept our age, to bloom where we are planted, to accept ourselves, and to be accepted as individuals gives strength to continue to live full and productive lives. We cannot change the fact that we are aging. Viktor Frankl advised that when there is nothing that we think can be done to change a situation, we can still change our attitude. Changing our attitude can help achieve one's full potential, including a sense of purpose, joy, love, and peace. To add value to the last thirty or forty years of life, it's important to change attitudes and to discard many superficial and material obsessions that only weigh us down. This is more difficult to do in very late life.

Psychological and social denial, individually and collectively, can be documented in almost every phase of the later years of life. Many use denial as a way of coping with anxiety. Denial patterns interfere with the acceptance of aging at all life stages, but especially in old age. Secretiveness about age and overuse of hair dyes, wigs, and cosmetics reflect a personal culturally determined need to appear young. Physical prowess is exaggerated. Such denials impede healthy adaptation to the reality of aging. A person's defensiveness toward his own aging may well be a dynamic predictor of late-life inability to adapt (Gaitz and Varner 1980).

Generativity is suggested by Erik Erikson (Erikson, Erikson, and Kivnik 1986) as the next-to-last stage of the life development cycle. This developmental stage involves the ability to support others—particularly one's children and other members of younger generations, caring and concern for younger people, and an interest in making a contribution to the world in which one lives. Stagnation results when we lack interest in others, feel we have contributed nothing, and are just going through the motions.

It is the meaning that one attributes to life and one's entire system of values that defines the value of old age. The reverse also applies. According to Simone de Beauvoir in *The Coming of Age*, "The way that a society behaves toward its old people

14

uncovers the naked and often carefully hidden truth about its real principles and aims" (1970, 85). It is the duty of society to enhance the lives of older adults by providing stimulating programs and experiences, meaningful employment, and optimal health care to allow access to growth and participation. Millions of baby boomer surveys indicate the desire of continued activity in the workforce and in the community (Freedman 2007). To seize this second wind, society's leaders and aging adults must combine forces to prepare for long and desirable, productive and joyful lives that will provide "triumphant movements" for our aging populations.

Ego integrity versus despair, the final developmental stage of life as described by Erikson, is all too often not achieved by many older adults. Despair is the result of rejecting one's life and oneself. Integrity, like the final movement of a great symphony, describes the harvest, "when the important themes of life" come together. When we can accept who we are (both the positive and the negative), what we have accomplished (having done the best one could do under the circumstances), and when we become responsible for the time remaining, we will have more opportunity to experience that triumphant movement. Late life will be a time of joy, not despair. The Peter Pan attitude that we will never grow old can hinder living a full and productive life.

— two —

SINKING

"And admit that the waters
Around you have grown
And accept it that soon
You'll be drenched to the bone.
If your time to you
Is worth savin'
Then you better start swimmin'
Or you'll sink like a stone"

Bob Dylan

This book is about aging well. The journey to the final movement of life's great symphony is less stressful when the components of the orchestra—the ups and downs connected with life's many experiences and the encounters

17

with persons along the way—have been satisfactorily resolved. The components of life are best orchestrated, decade by decade, encounter by encounter, before the sojourn on earth reaches its final stages.

On my way to aging well, it was not possible to evade many sorrowful and difficult experiences. One of the major contributions to my final movement of late life consisted of my learning how to cope with life's difficulties. My encounters with troubled women married to military men provided examples of how to learn to deal with life's complications. One unforgettable person, Jeanie, was married to a U.S. Army hospital commander who had been ordered to duty in Germany. Jeannie proved to be a real friend to me as I encountered problems living in Germany. When my own husband was ordered to Germany, we considered what was best for our children's education and we decided to keep them in their present schools in Georgia until the end of the school year; then we would join their father in Germany. This unexpected change of location provided time to downsize the household, to store and pack necessities, to complete my university program, to learn German, and to select colors for our future home to be painted before our arrival in Germany.

My two children (then ages twelve and sixteen) were very happy in their private school and they remained immersed in school activities while I focused my spare time on making plans to live abroad for several years. Months later, after frequent communication with my husband, we arrived in Germany and were alarmed to observe the psychological changes in him. He made it quite clear that we were not welcome; we should not have come because we were not wanted. Frustrated and ill from the negative experience, I began to think of how, as a total stranger in a new environment, I could make lemonade out of a lemon. Because of the unpleasant arrival (which my husband had enthusiastically promoted and planned), I began to look for a place to get away for a few days to review what had happened and to plan. I had successfully rented our stateside home, saw no feasible way to return immediately, and could not quite grasp how to cope with this new development. I knew no other person with whom to share my problem and did not know how to find help in a new foreign environment. I coped by writing numerous letters to my family—some were mailed, some were not. My meeting another doctor's wife, Jeanie, turned out to be mutually beneficial.

Jeannie and I became good friends; she knew more than I did about how to navigate the military bureaucracy, and she shared personal information about her marriage with me. She told me that it had never been a happy one. I shared with her the trauma with which I was coping, and the fact that although my marriage was not a happy one, once the children were born, I had to focus on what was best for them. I had been extremely close to my in-laws, whom I loved and highly respected and with whom I had warm relationships. I was not concerned about my own well-being, even though at a previous time I had actually called the military police in Georgia for protection. I had to get away to think and, at the same time, to distract the children with a new experience. Jeanie helped me locate the travel bureau close to where we were temporarily quartered and I purchased an inexpensive trip to London for a few days. The children were happy with new experiences while I had time to try to reflect on what was going on.

Returning from England to Germany, I became immersed in the children's education and the German community. I took advantage of opportunities to use my limited German and I met Germans via my daughter's piano lessons with a private music teacher. Through this teacher's affiliation I arranged a cross-cultural musical exchange program between the American military community and the local German community. This involvement that connected the children with the German community proved to be beneficial later with the military commanding general. Also, my son had become friends with the son of the American elementary school principal and he enjoyed the relationship with both the son and his father. My children and I attended the local chapel, where we met other American military people. Through church relationships, we became close friends with one family. My husband did not participate in any family activities, although this was not unusual. I suspected that he had become involved with a cocktail waitress at the military bar, but I did not pursue it. I was busy playing double parental roles, trying to compensate for the strange, unanticipated behavior of their father, and to adjust to a foreign environment during the daytime and a stressful private one in the evenings. He drank moderately at the time and was usually absorbed in himself; he spent most of his time at home wearing earphones and listening to music. He was not approachable.

Just a few months after our arrival in Germany, and after the children were settled in new schools, I received a phone call from the military hospital; my husband was expected to leave the country immediately—he was being transferred again, this time to a research position in Alabama. This was his second unexpected, immediate transfer. Alarmed, but familiar with the commanding general who had issued the order, I left our quarters and drove immediately to the general's office, stormed past the attache's office, and asked the general what was happening and why. He, his wife, and other officer families had been invited for lunch at our quarters the Sunday before this happened. The general explained that the doctor's behavior had been followed for several years and that he did not feel that the doctor was an appropriate representative of the military command in a foreign country. He would be returned to a stateside position until he could receive his twenty-year military retirement, only one year ahead. This was a benevolent solution for him, but what about me and the children?

At my request, I was granted permission to remain in Germany until the children finished the school year. Surprised that I was granted this privilege, in spite of the hasty departure of our sponsor, I retained all the rights of a military dependent, though we were downsized to a smaller set of quarters. Very grateful to the commanding general, I took advantage of many opportunities of living on foreign soil. Our sponsor, my husband, departed; he requested that we end our marriage upon our return to the states. I set in motion the divorce process through legal recommendations of friends and family back home.

Experiences that I wanted to share with the children while still in Europe included visiting Berlin to see the Berlin Wall. We were allowed to ride the American troop train, to cross over into the East Zone, and to purchase books and coins. My son loved being part of the military experience. Often he was the only son of a "bird" colonel, and was allowed privileges that were very appealing to a twelve-year-old boy. We had priority seating and attention on the troop train, as well as on the plane when we finally flew back to the states. These final military privileges were enriching and opened new doors for the three of us.

As an instructor with the University of Maryland European Division (in Heidelberg, Germany) I had become quite fluent in the German language. I began to translate for Americans when we were traveling on German transportation. Jeanie and I visited cultural events nearby and had ample opportunity to share stories while our children chatted with each other and became good friends. Both of us were married to physicians, both of us were in unhappy marriages, and both of us had two adolescent children.

I wanted to learn to ski, and wanted my children to have the experience as well. Still a military dependent, it was afford-able through the facilities we could access. I had never been exposed to skiing on snow, having only waterskied on Tennessee lakes. The children readily took to the sport, but I had great difficulty getting the long strips of metal under control. I must have been a pitiful sight, because observers would offer to help me. One of those observers, an American civilian working in Germany, actually enticed me to get on the ski lift behind him and try to sky downhill with him. He was so sure that he could teach me how to handle the skis—I only needed "momentum." Mistake number one! He also forgot to tell me how to get *off* the lift. At the end of the lift ride, I didn't know what to do, but my German was good enough that I understood the Germans yelling at me—*Fallen Sie!* ("Fall Off!") I fell off into a mountain of snow and was not very receptive when my newly acquainted teacher came to help me down the mountain—carrying my skis. Trying to compensate for his lack of judgment, he offered to help me ship all my household goods, sell the car, and make all other arrangements for departure as soon as school was out. I assumed that that was supposed to compensate for a face full of snow and lost pride, but the encounter proved to have been a valuable one in the next few months. Because of his affiliation with American intelligence, he knew more about me than was comfortable. He could verify who I was.

During this first sojourn in Germany, I often felt uneasy in a foreign environment. Relating to the trauma of my friend Jeanie, with whom I had developed a caring relationship, I felt blessed to be there for her and to share our mutual feelings. However, both of us were Southern women, and in the seventies divorce was a last resort. We discussed this over tea several times.

In spite of the questionable quality of educational opportunities for Americans living abroad, both of my children found their way through the school year without, at least, observable damage. There were opportunities to go to the German schools, but I resisted because I felt they would be better trained in familiar American-style school environments for such a brief and difficult time.

They finished the year with honors at their respective schools for Americans abroad and military dependents. I continued to learn German and the process for shipping a full household back to Georgia. When the packers came, they stole my jewelry and oriental carpets, in spite of my watchful eye. Once out of sight, valuables were taken before boxes were boarded up and shipped by sea. I was beginning to live with loss.

My husband wanted a divorce; he often mentioned a college sweetheart he had admired, but who had shown little or no interest in him. He had kept up with her and knew that she had recently become widowed. I kept my focus on the future and began to qualify for employment. I had spent life up to this point as mother and father to my two children, complying with all the distaff duties of wife and community leader.

I wrote Georgia State University and requested permission to attend their Studies Abroad in German Program at the Friedrich-Alexander University of Nürnberg, not far from where we were located. Having completed the Spanish Abroad Studies in Madrid much earlier in my educational experience, I was immediately accepted and given a special student rate in the Georgia program in Germany because I was already on site. I had only to find my own housing near Nuernberg University. I was later joined in Nuernberg by fifteen students from Georgia. We spent the summer studying German, and I graduated with enough hours to qualify to teach German. This success strengthened my confidence to begin employment in a field of study then required by many high schools, study of a foreign language.

Returning to Georgia from our first sojourn in Germany, court proceedings were not necessary. My husband had promoted a divorce without going to court; he signed legal documents, I complied, and with that, twenty years of married life came to a close. Life after divorce began, and I didn't have many resources, especially employment experience. I felt alone and ostracized by some of my friends—especially one of my neighbors who had been my closest friend. What made life bearable was two wonderful children and their paternal grandfather. He called me and offered the following: cancellation of any debt, the car, and a generous trust fund for the children's education. The paternal grandparents had loaned us money, gifted us with a car, and with a down payment on the house—it even remained in my possession. Encouraged by this endorsement of my responsibility to their grandchildren, I took every job I could find to continue to maintain the expenses of private schools and limited diversions. I budgeted carefully and found enough funding for a master's degree at a nearby college that would improve my qualifications for teacher employment.

Forty years ago, divorce still carried a stigma, especially in the South. However, the saddest aspect of my situation was the pain it must have inflicted on the paternal grandparents, who had been the best two grandparents anyone could wish. I missed them very much, and my challenge was to care for their grandchildren as they would wish, although under trying circumstances. I was thrilled when my daughter chose to go to Vanderbilt University, very near the grandparents' home.

Both Jeanie and I kept in touch via phone and letters, and she began to communicate with her Mississippi friends about her future. Meantime, I was overwhelmed with the adjustments that a single mom faces, but I had not forgotten my Mississippi friend, and we shared the blow-by-blow challenges of two middle-aged women with adolescent children.

I looked for employment in Georgia, and the children returned to their private school in Savannah. The next three years went relatively smoothly. I found a job immediately, and we were quite comfortable back in our modest Savannah home, within walking distance of the children's school. My language abilities qualified me for teaching English as a second language, Spanish, and German. I was not yet certified to work in the public schools; ironically, I was immediately employed as a teacher at the local military post and worked part time at the military post exchange as a cashier. I took an Avon job in the community, selling cosmetics in the evening. With several jobs and the child support I received, plus the generosity of my former in-laws, we were able to maintain our standard of living. I soon began a master's degree program at Georgia Southern University, keeping very busy trying to improve my earning capacity by earning my teaching certificate.

Rage against my former husband crept into my nightmares, but I dedicated all my waking hours to study and to making life comfortable for my children. I never thought about dating, although opportunities were presented. Responsibilities of a single mom were heavy, and although remembering the Greek tragedies (especially the Medea tragedy and the rage and destruction following the abandonment of the Queen by her husband), the enraged memories of my husband never went further than to pour all his alcoholic beverages down the drain. That did give me a sort of sadistic pleasure! My past was drained away.

About a year after our return from Germany, I received a surprise phone call from Morocco on my birthday. Good grief! It was the guy on the ski slopes in Germany who had tried to help me learn to ski. He was still on loan by a civilian agency to the military in Germany, and was professionally employed in a career that allowed him to trace Americans abroad. He knew more about me than one would expect and he wanted to come to Georgia to visit us. My response was "If you are serious, call me back in two years. I am too busy for guests now, and I want nothing to interfere with the children's activities." What a shock when he waited two years and called back!

He was "allowed" to visit two years later, just as my daughter left for her graduation cruise to the Bahamas. He, my son, and I had a very enjoyable visit touring the local Savannah restaurants, sites, and visiting with friends. The oppressive summer heat was quite a change from Germany and from his Montana home, but he truly enjoyed the visit. He returned to Germany after a week and when he transferred planes in London, he called and asked if I would marry him. My startled answer— "I might." He told me that he was a bachelor, but we had had only very brief times together and I had to do some checking on him! I soon learned that he had no perceptible baggage, and that he really was single. I was forty years old and if the news about him continued to be good, then I was interested.

three

SURFING AND MAKING LEMONADE

"If an architect wants to strengthen a decrepit arch, they increase the load that is laid upon it..."

Viktor Frankl

Scuba diving is an unforgettable experience. Surfing from the depths of the ocean, from the coral reefs, surrounded by tropical fish and various types of ocean foliage, one surfaces from a beautiful world to the beauty of the other world we live in. I had often scuba dived off the island of Oahu during a year-long sojourn in Hawaii. After the phone call from the "instructor," I suddenly felt as if I were surfing from the depths of responsibility and loneliness that I had shouldered alone for the past three years of unanticipated single status, and from a previous very difficult marriage.

Looking back, I had suppressed a lot of drives through physical activity when the family had lived in Hawaii. I took up swimming and scuba as well as hula and the ukulele. At this stage, my daughter was in a private kindergarten; while she was in school, my son and I went swimming daily. In the evenings, I took scuba diving with eleven other men, including my first husband, the Army flight surgeon. At the ocean test of our scuba course, all of us dove off Kaneohe, the leeward side of Oahu. Ten of us returned; my husband was missing. Hopelessly wringing my hands, nobody seemed to know what to do. I jumped in my car, drove to the nearest Hawaiian home, and asked to use their phone. I called the emergency services at the hospital he commanded and requested a helicopter to search for the doctor.

By the time I arrived back at the diving cliff where our dive had begun, the helicopter was landing. My husband had consumed his usual breakfast of eggs and sausage before diving, against recommendations. He had become nauseated in the rough waters and had succumbed to the Molokai rip tide. He didn't fight the tide, but rode it out, saving his life by saving sufficient strength to swim back to shore, just as the helicopter landed.

Meanwhile, back in Savannah after the phone call from Morocco, I began to relive the scuba experience and the euphoria that one experiences in tropical waters, surrounded by the flora and fauna in clear blue water and coral-lined reefs. I was feeling this familiar euphoria because someone had found me and my children desirable. I had felt lonely and rejected as a single mom, but had sublimated my frustrations into self-improvement via education. The children had really liked the ski instructor, and at my age, I felt that I did not want to spend the rest of my life alone. My daughter was ready for college and my son was in high school. After several more phone calls from the instructor and much new information about him from my students at the Savannah military location, I entertained an interest in remarriage. I had met, through my first real job at the military post in Savannah, men who had known our civilian ski instructor, and their opinions were carefully measured. I confirmed through my adult students that he was single, had no children, and was "somewhat eccentric." Six months later, he returned to Savannah for a second visit, which provided time to get to know each other better. The two adult children were very receptive to his visits and were resilient enough to accept another adult man in their lives without alienation from their biological father, or so it seemed at the time. We were later married at a small community church, with my children attending and my brother, Ray, performing the ceremony, and my father, D. T. McCall, giving me away—again!

With my daughter immersed in her pre-med studies at Vanderbilt, and my son quite willing to return to Germany for a happier and more productive visit, we packed and stored household goods again. Germany became my home for the second time—for a longer and happier visit. My second husband successfully continued to be recontracted with his civilian employer. My son adjusted readily again to the Munich dependent school for civilians working abroad and for military dependents. I was quite fearful that the new marriage would damage my son's development, and I tried everything I knew to make the adjustment positive for both son and husband. Tejas, the family dog, had accompanied us, and although my husband wasn't happy about that, he tolerated the dog. One day, I thought the dog had soiled the carpet. The smell was of strong urine. I searched for a yellow spot but could not find it, then opened all the windows to air the apartment. The open windows only increased the smell. Puzzled, I ran outside to ask the landlady where the odor might be coming from. She laughed while explaining that the farmers were spraying the crops with *kuhmist,* a collection of cow urine that was used as natural fertilizer. There was no other crisis of this type with the dog, until one evening it became ill and we rushed to a German veterinarian. Completely confident that I could handle the conversation with the vet, I was shocked that I did not understand his German. To my astonishment, my husband did understand the Bavarian dialect—a musical, soft dialect of the standard language that I comprehended.

I applied for substitute teaching in my son's school in Munich, where I was soon offered a full-time position. I taught there long enough to learn that the educational level was less than what would qualify him to gain entrance to the college he preferred. After just one year in the dependent's school, my son and I returned to Savannah where he resumed his former education. He graduated with honors and received a scholarship to Wake Forest University. I returned to Germany and rejoined my husband. Experiencing the empty nest syndrome, I perfected my language skills, entered the German University and dove into the challenges of scientific German literature. With total dedication to learn all that I could, in an expected tour of several years, I adjusted well to the challenges. To earn money to augment the financial support of the children, I worked part time as a German teacher and counselor for the U.S. Army in Europe.

We remained there beyond the four years required for me to complete all resident seminar requirements for my doctorate. I might add that I had become very happy with my second husband, who worked the midnight-to-8AM shift at the local American facility. His schedule freed me for copious hours to pursue my dream: a doctorate in the German language. Meantime, many unforgettable experiences are logged in our scrapbook of memories of those years.

At the time we lived there, the Bader-Meinhoff terrorist group was active in Germany. One stormy, snowy night, our car refused to start and there was no alternative to get to work, except to walk. Wrapped up like an Eskimo, my husband began a ten kilometer walk to work at midnight. Stopped by the German police, who assumed that he was a member of the terrorist group (his face was covered with a black mask to protect against the cold), he was ordered into the police wagon. How fortunate for him because the *polizei* took him to work in their warm van, but only after his ID proved that he was an American and with the assurance that the military police at the military post would identify him as a civilian working for the military.

We finally left Germany—before I finished my dissertation. That was completed and returned, chapter by chapter in German, to my "Doktor Vater Professor" at the University. My final education-related trip to Germany was three years later, to face three professors, one in each of three different departments, for my oral doctoral examination. I had spent the three days previous to the exams in a cold guest room of a Bavarian couple, studying night and day for the examinations. My hearing had not yet deteriorated to a level that made the auditory exams unclear, but the questions in German were challenging. In retrospect, I am mystified that I pulled it off. With magna cum laude honors, I received my title as "Frau Doktor" a few months later.

The party for me after the oral examinations was at my Doktor Vater's home, but I was very ill by the time I stepped off the Munich *ubahn* (subway) at his home. I later learned that I had been suffering from Selye's Stress Syndrome. The professor's pharmacist daughter had come to my farewell party and had given me some medication that was effective; I did not embarrass anyone during the party! The professor's family became lifelong friends, and we have since visited several times.

My doctorate had been very challenging, but the divorce had been my most trying adjustment in life. I had grown up in a traditional family, a strongly religious one where marriage was sacred and forever. The children had been, like the priority of my mother and my paternal in-laws, the anchor of my life. However, my first husband never enjoyed being with my parents and siblings, and although not popular, he was always welcomed and tolerated by my family. Family support for my remarriage was very positive and helpful.

This change of direction in my life, and in the lives of my children, has been positive and stimulating. In retrospect, I am grateful for the doctor's earlier decision to break the marriage vows. My life for the subsequent thirty plus years has been challenging and rewarding.

I would hardly ever recommend divorce, but can assure the reader that sometimes it is unavoidable. When difficulties are not resolvable, the adjustment process can be painful, but as is true with the aging process, changes that are forced upon us—whether biological, psychological, professional, or social—can be turned to advantage. My experience as the seventh child in a large, poorly-educated family had provided a training ground for the development of coping skills and for living successfully in a dysfunctional marital relationship. The exposure to the difficulties of German women who had survived two world wars, yet remained positive and productive, had given me confidence. As one of my projects at the German university, I had interviewed many older German women about survival under trying times. Many of them had quoted Nietsche, "*Wenn es mich nicht totet, es macht mich staerker.*" (If it doesn't kill me, it makes me stronger!) (Frankl 1984, 109). That had become my motto for overcoming personal dilemmas and for meeting the challenges of matriculation in a foreign university as an older American.

The route to developing coping and decision-making skills was long, and not always simple. In a troubled marriage, but with determination to survive, previous experiences had provided ample opportunities to learn how to cope with difficulties.

Meantime, while checking on my old friend, Jeanie, I learned she had decided to end her marriage many months before. During the remaining time with her husband in Germany she became pregnant. Frightened by the responsibility of bringing another child into a deteriorating marriage, she sought an abortion. With the father's approval and encouragement, she developed a plan to acquire a safe, respectable way to end the pregnancy. Her husband accompanied her to consult with a local private physician. They told him of the marriage problems and of her need for help with uterine pain and bleeding—she needed a D and C (Dilation and Curettage: this is the removal from the uterus of any remains of conception).

The local doctor agreed to perform the minor surgery, but he did not realize that Jeanie was pregnant, nor did he perform any tests to determine that. He advised her to return for the surgery and to bring a urine sample. This was clearly negligence on his part, but with a physician husband present, he did not follow normal procedures nor question their request.

Fully aware that she was pregnant, but also aware that the consulting physician might not proceed if he knew it, she shared her problem with her best female friend. The friend agreed to give Jeanie her own personal urine sample to substitute for Jeanie's. It worked. The doctor, who had ill-advisedly not taken a sample when she visited him, tested the sample and proceeded with the D and C. He was supposedly surprised when he told her that he had discovered a fetus during the surgery, but could not reverse the procedure. Jeanie never knew what the surgeon really knew—whether he had been aware of what was going on, or whether he was aware and just didn't want to challenge her husband, a high-ranking military physician. Jeanie called me shortly after this, weeping and grief stricken. I consoled her with the impossibility of reversing the procedure, but that changing her attitude, which was still in her control, was necessary to move on for her children's sake.

Later, Jeanie told me that she never regretted her decision to proceed with the surgery. She could take care of two children—one on each hand—but the future of playing both parental roles was too problematic. Without professional qualifications for employment, the strength to cope with upheaval after upheaval of change and unexpected new adjustments, physically and mentally, it seemed to be the right decision at the time. She was also a military dependent, without adequate professional training or skills. Her husband had become increasingly abusive, verbally and physically. The handwriting was on the wall, but she was too insecure to move out. She did not wish to disgrace her family as the first divorcee in a religious and historically-proud Southern family. In retrospect, both she and I went through some very tough times, but they didn't kill us; they made us stronger, and much more compassionate. She did not reveal the abortion to anyone except to me, her helpful neighborhood friend, and her husband. I supported her psychologically during the aftermath of her expressed guilt feelings, and believed it was probably the right decision for her under the circumstances, as did her friend who collaborated with her actions. Her friend had long since observed a very difficult family environment.

41

Following this experience with Jeanie and my own experience with a physician, I lost respect for many physicians because of their abuse of power and the status unquestionably granted them. In my experience working in a medical college, I have quite recently encountered unethical actions involving young, beautiful women who are attracted to a white coat.

Aging well requires coping with each difficult issue to the best of our ability and forgiving ourselves when later insight might have led to other alternatives. Support from family and friends can make the difference when trouble arises. My family and my mutual sharing of experiences with Jeanie made possible the changes from a dysfunctional relationship to a later life of quality and high productivity. Aging well requires that we resolve problems as we go through life and accept the decisions that we made to resolve them. Carrying them forward will weigh us down and interfere with future development and adjustments.

— four —

MIDLIFE IN PERSPECTIVE— EDIT OR REGRET IT!

"Full maturity . . . is achieved by realizing that you have a choice to make."

Angela Barron McBride

Why do we think of midlife as a crisis? Is it grey hair, wrinkles, reading glasses, *or* is it taking stock? Is it the responsibility of being caught in the middle; being both parent and child—helping adolescent children grow up and helping aging parents make adjustments and changes? Is it the realization that we haven't achieved what we could have, and we wonder if there is enough time left?

When the big forty is celebrated and the big fifty makes one aware that a half-century of life has elapsed, panic sets in.

Many experience a crisis. Our culture has not prepared us for the last half-century of life that many will experience. Our idea of a good old age can be accomplishments such as biking across America, looking like Oprah or Jane Fonda, or climbing the Himalayas. Many have made no effort to clarify a prospective style of life different from the first half-century of our lives. There are no role prescriptions for the last half-century of life. In our mortality-ridden society we don't plan to live long, yet there are indications that many of us will reach one hundred. Dr. Walter Bortz confirms that humans have the potential to live one hundred twenty years or longer. Although only a few of us will reach that advanced age, many of us have the potential to live past what the insurance agencies predict—an average of seventy-five years. If you have ever looked at the back of your birth certificate, your expiration date is one hundred years. If you "expire" before then, it is not necessarily because you are old, but rather because something in the environment (accidents, pollution) or in your lifestyle may have caused your demise (Bortz 2007).

A great deal of responsibility for what we become in old age rests with the individual at midlife. The majority of conditions in later life are under our control, and cannot be attributed to genetics (Bortz 2007). It is particularly important to reprioritize in midlife. Although we must deal with physical, psychological, and social changes, how we face them is determined by our response to them; they are not pre-determined. We cannot rush through life until we burn out, or run out of time; we must prioritize.

Common sense tells us that aging is universal, inevitable, and associated with gradual physical decline. Scientists now challenge this common sense. Some animal species do not appear to age at all. Within the last decade, biologists have found that the rate of aging is remarkably easy to alter in certain lab animals. We know that it may not be possible to extend life, but that it is definitely possible to extend youth. It may not be possible to suddenly shrivel away at the end—like Dracula when exposed to the sunlight—but it is possible to enjoy the sun's rays much longer and in good health.

What has changed is the development of a theory about the evolution of aging with real explanatory power and conceptual beauty. There are now enough elderly in good health to reassure us that getting old is not synonymous with becoming ill or disabled. Although progressive inefficiency in maintaining homeostatic balance (keeping all the body's systems working smoothly) is challenging, along with taking charge of our health account and assuming responsibility (as we do of our bank account), starting early enough and prioritizing time and energy resources, we can definitely extend youth and delay disease. If we wish to live better, as well as longer, just knowing about the trends in the potential length of life can stimulate plans to improve our health account. The Swedish national demographic date from 1961 to 1991 indicated that during that time period the maximum age at death rose from 101 to 108. Ever-optimistic Californians suggest that the average female could achieve an expected life of one hundred years, if just one of our major killers could be eliminated (Bortz 2007).

We cannot deny that whatever gets broken is increasingly hard to fix. Prevention is important for the young; it is critical in middle-age. The middle years are no time for reckless disregard of maintenance of mind and body. Some turn to medicine to avoid challenges, but medicine can make patients out of normal people. Although it is never too late to make adjustments, it is easier in midlife to correct directions and to change unhealthy behavior. Getting old is like visiting a foreign country: the more we prepare for it, the more enjoyable it will be. We would not travel without checking our bank account; growing older without checking our health account is equally foolhardy. So, we reprioritize at age fifty when 40 percent or more of our life remains. We answer questions about where we are, where we are going, and why. We follow Socrates's advice that the unexamined life is not worth living. If we examine our lives before we age, the long trip ahead can be much more pleasant. We begin by repairing relationships, discarding guilt, forgiving others, living in the present, and moving into the future without a heavy load. Preparation to deal with the inevitable adjustments is absolutely essential: physical changes, psychological adjustments, career adaptations, and stock-taking. The key need at this time and later is the ability to adapt to, and cope with, the difficulties of life. Using the advanced common sense unique to older adults, we become able to discern "why and what for" instead of asking "how" to get through life's perils (Frankl 1984).

Time is of the essence; we must use it wisely. However, we humans don't do very well with time. Dr. Walter Bortz has noted that only humans are aware that they have a future; other members of the animal species are not (Bortz 2007). But, why then do we fail to plan for the future as we age? Many feel that in midlife time is their enemy. Instead of using their past as a springboard to the future, they remain focused on the past, on aging, and on decline.

When one becomes aware that life is limited and that the past cannot be changed, denial of inevitable aging only makes conditions worse. The challenges of unanticipated changes in midlife can result in internal criticism. Relationships with one's children, changes in health, increased sensitivity to stress, tiring easily, and other changes challenge coping strategies. A feeling of worthlessness in one's career or a forced retirement can increase questioning one's own personality and worth.

Midlife crisis is the confrontation with the unavoidable loss of power—a total loss of self. The importance of the many changes in the stages of life before age sixty-five should not be underestimated. The resources to change are still available; knowledge about aging can help with adjustments.

This phase can be a type of testing ground for later life crises. This phase of life, exactly like the phase of puberty, has a high potential for self-integration and further development, or—on the other hand—for stagnation and doubt. Once change is accepted and problems are resolved, the self-image is strengthened. One is more capable of self-determination and is more open to giving free rein to the imagination, as well as to discarding the opinions and patterns of society. One can concentrate on new tasks, the learning process, and the ability for self-expression. This process, however, must develop from self-confidence and understanding within the individual in order to meet the challenges of behavioral change. Through strengthening and changes of self-image, a person succeeds in gaining more flexibility. This can empower one to change goals and to increase personal growth through education and new experiences. It is much easier in middle age than in later life to question one's personality and values, and to overcome defensiveness and regression, while still having a relatively positive appreciation of, and attitude toward, one's body. For these reasons, middle age is a very important period for ensuring successful aging (Rosenmayr 1981).

The aging process begins early, and one must deal with ongoing stress and limited energy. Developing skills needed to achieve a good quality of life should be started early. Time and practice are required to change habits. We must learn how to change habits before we have a crisis. We can even change the brain by adjusting our routines. When one no longer has the ability to cope with changes, the lack of physical energy and the onset of potentially frail conditions can collide with achieving personal goals. Thanks to modern medicine, many middle-aged persons retain their physical and mental health. Therefore, middle age is really the best time to take the necessary steps to prepare for the future.

There are basic discontinuities in our lives from age fifty to age one hundred. We focus on preserving youthful looks and status, we fritter away precious time in front of the television set, we analyze what's wrong with others, and we consider cosmetic surgery. In short, we make a natural stage of life very complicated and troublesome, instead of opening our hearts and minds to new experiences with the expectation of a long and productive journey.

Realistically, the expectation of becoming a centenarian can increase our chances of achieving a longer life. Expectation is a vital dynamic. In areas of the world where prestige is enhanced by long life, the expectation of longevity makes living longer more likely. When Alexander Leaf and his team from Boston searched for persons claiming to be one hundred sixty years old in former Soviet Georgia and the Caucus Mountains, he could not verify anyone older than one hundred, but found a lot of very healthy older people who aspired to be one hundred. Those claiming to be one hundred forty to one hundred sixty years old had fraudulently documented an older age because it was prestigious; it was considered a great achievement. Leaf reported that these older people did not suffer from obesity, cancer, or heart disease and lived on average to be one hundred years old (Leaf 1973). Planning to live a long life may have led to healthier habits that improved the quality of life. In his book *Healthy at 100* (2007), John Robbins documents the advantages of many Pigmy, Hunza, and other cultures where long lives are anticipated. His focus on the importance of love in achieving longevity adds to the documented research of life-lengthening good nutrition, regular exercise, sleep, and ongoing socialization.

Frustration at midlife could be based on the false assumption that retirement and aging are synonymous. We see retirement as the beginning of the end of life. However, middle age (40–59) precedes retirement; retirement (ages 60–75) foreshadows aging; aging foreshadows death (76–120). Some physicians claim that if we live healthfully, we have no reason to decline before age eighty, when some organs begin to show wear and tear.

We have a new role to play in midlife, a different one from our earlier roles. It requires a focus on re-prioritizing. The transitional phases of life can be the most meaningful. Life is change, change is ongoing, and the flexibility to change is maturity. Change allows for constant re-creation of oneself.

A profitable route toward reinvention of oneself is to reenter the work force and, as the economy declines, an increasing number of older women are doing that. Annual averages of labor-force participation rates of women age fifty-five and older from 2004–2005 showed an increase. Women over age seventy increased in the workforce from 6.7 percent to 7.1. Labor force participation of men also increased, with men age seventy and over increasing from 12.8 percent in 2004 to 13.5 percent in 2005 (Washington 2006). Although retirement ages have changed for those born after 1938, the general trend is still to retire as soon as possible. Since we are becoming healthier and the disability rates in later life are slowly falling, we are certainly capable of continued productivity. We are more likely to achieve the triumphant last movement that the pope talked about if we achieve wholeness. Wholeness—exhibited by gratitude for life, being remembered, having charity, grace, compassion, resourcefulness, and meaning—is easier to achieve when we stay connected, either through work or community participation.

In midlife we must consider how to avoid brokenness or despairing, characterized by meaninglessness, greed, guilt, apathy, self-condemnation, loneliness, and revenge. One essential way to do this is to focus on mental and physical health because the quality of life we desire will not be possible without good health.

The most challenging years for good health appear in middle age, when our physiological systems are changing and adjusting. This is known as the "crossover phenomenon" in some groups. We are more susceptible to major changes, but if we cross over this period in good health, we have achieved a major step on the road to a higher quality of life in later life.

We want life to be understandable, so we want to discard rigid, ingrained patterns of behavior. We can profit from changes to our comforting patterns of life. At midlife we must plan for re-firement, instead of retirement; for life preview, instead of life review. A little tension between what we are, what we have become, and what we potentially can become will help prepare us for Ger-rassic Park (Dychtwald and Flower 1989).

We have a new role to play; a different one from our earlier roles. If we have not learned how to cope with problems in our youth, we must now develop a "repair mentality" for growing old. Our status is no longer determined by the things that used to determine status—it's where we are in life that matters, not where or what we have been. As we enter middle age and as we change our priorities, my mom used to say that every human contact is a piece of eternity. People become more important as we mature; increased social capital is a great asset.

Basically, at midlife our role is roleless, unstructured by society; there is no foundation for viable social motives. We must be pioneers; our role must be seen as legitimate and valuable.

Attitude change is imperative. When we give up previous status in exchange for a new one, motivation to meet the challenges of midlife is more likely to occur. Teens anxiously await age sixteen because they will be permitted to drive; age twenty-one is anticipated because alcohol can be legally consumed; at age twenty-five, car insurance rates decline. Age defines many aspects of life, and it advances in one direction only: forward. Each new stage brings negatives and positives, and we learn to cope at each new age.

The late Jules Willing used the example of a space launch to explain what the last stages of life can be. At a space launch, the monstrous, powerful force of the booster rockets have only one purpose—to go higher and faster. During the launch all the energy is expended, driving forward and upward. The space capsule ship sits quietly atop the rocket, seemingly having no function at all—it is, so to speak, dormant. When the boosters are finished and the proper altitude is reached, the boosters fall away—their task finished. The space capsule comes alive now—it can change direction, move into any altitude, all the while traveling faster than the boosters. It is free of restraints; it has some control. It can link itself to others and provide views never seen before. It is in a foreign land, but it is prepared. Systems analysts had developed plans for what would happen when the powerful boosters had finished their tasks (Willing 1981). Likewise,

we must plan for what will happen when our youthful energies decline.

Midlife is a time of preparation, a holistic preparation. There
should be no regret in dropping the first stage of life—our
careers, letting our children go, and helping them grow—the
best preparation for their aging. With forethought and planning,
we will be launched into a new stage of life that is peaceful,
joyful, and without regret. We gain control, freedom, changed
values—new purposes and goals that are appropriate for the
latter stages of life, that are rooted in whatever value system
we have at the time. They are clearly different from previous
goals and values. There is no map for this new game; the key
is anticipating the inevitability of change. We will then be free
for the next stage of our lifelong journey—to explore our inner
selves and to find our outer limits (Willing 1981). Preparing
for and learning to grow old may be more difficult than
growing up. There may be much to reprioritize when habits are
ingrained; starting before we arrive eases the changes.
Opportunities to prepare for the years after retirement are
fleeting. In midlife we still have the resources to change the
things that might not be beneficial in later life.

I am reminded of a story that I once heard about death: a
good, conscientious, young man came to the aid of a weak and

dying man on the street. The victim, who had been beaten by a robber, gathered strength to speak. He asked the young man "Do you know who I am? I am Death. I will have to take you when your time is up, but because you have been so kind, I will give you a warning before I return to take you with me."

The young man went about his life as most of us do. He married, had children, retired, traveled, and worked around the house in his spare time. One day, he was repairing the roof when the ladder on which he stood collapsed. He broke almost every bone in his body. In intense pain, he waited for help. When no one came immediately, he began to weep and to fear that he was dying. Before he went into shock, he remembered that Death had promised him a warning before taking him away.

After an extended recovery from the fall, he suffered from another illness, which was accompanied by a very high fever. Burning with fever, he again remembered that Death had promised him a warning.

The next year he suffered from a sudden onset of gout. One night after a hard day of yard work, the pain was excruciating. He felt that he would die, but was comforted by the fact that Death had promised him a warning.

He miraculously recovered, and on a warm spring day he went for a walk in the park. Someone tapped him on the shoulder. The stranger said, "I am Death, and I have come to take you with me."

"But you promised me that there would be a warning," insisted the young man.

"But I did warn you—three times. Remember the fall, the fever, and the gout?"

Most of us live as if we will be around forever; we ignore the warnings. Yet, the uncertainty of life demands consideration. Any one of us could go for a walk on Sunday, and be beyond medical intervention on Thursday. Death may not give us warnings. Victor Frankl did give us an admonition: "Live as if you were living for the second time and if you acted the first time as wrongly as you are about to act now" (Frankl 1984, 114). If we lived by Immanuel Kant's categorical imperative we wouldn't need any warnings: "Act only on that maxim through which you can, at the same time, will that it should become a universal law." Kant meant that when we act, regardless of how insignificant it may seem, we should think of what the consequences would be if every other person felt free to act in the same manner.

We may not have the opportunity to enjoy our earthly existence a second time. This is why we must plan for the last decades of our lives. We can overcome the time limitation in one way: by burning time. The poet Yeats expressed this very notion:

The innocent and the beautiful

Have no enemy but time

Arise and bid me strike a match

And strike a match til time catch . . . (Bianchi 1982, 146).

Yeats wrote the poem to eulogize two sisters. He told how they had set time afire by intensely using it for good purposes. Yeats states that "the true significance of these women rests in the intensity of their commitment to the causes of mankind" (Bianchi 1982, 147). Yeats challenges us to set time afire, as if the length of our days were insignificant. In *Aging as a Spiritual Journey*, Bianchi describes how the two sisters' commitment to causes that benefit humankind was burning time. He explains that the "ability to burn time, to relativize it, becomes a kind of spiritual alchemy that reduces the sheer material weight and extension of your years. It is a process of refining the gold of our lives . . . to ennoble the golden years with the quality of soul that has been distilled" (Ibid.).

It's true that from midlife on we are pioneers on a new trip. Preparation for the journey to late life includes physical, emotional, rational, social (family, friends, and community), and financial fitness. The aging process occurs slowly over many decades and the remaining time will be fulfilling if we plan ahead.

Most of us already know what we must do to remain healthy. Good health is the underpinning for maximum development. We know that we should exercise. The problem is with accountability. Two-thirds of seniors over age sixty-five do not exercise adequately for good health. Yet studies continue to reinforce the fact that an unfit person of thirty is in the same physical condition as a fit person at age seventy. The Dallas Bed Study, the Harvard Health Study, the Aging and Disability Study by Leveille, and the Swedish studies by Saavborfg reinforce the "move it or lose it" idea (Garrett 1998).

Seventy-five percent of us do not eat right, yet 85 percent of our diseases are nutritionally related. Habits and culture prevent us from consuming nutrient-dense calories (fruits and vegetables) instead of calorie-dense foods (doughnuts and other unnatural sweets). Our government cannot fix these problems; money is not the solution—behavioral change is!

Do we get our check-ups and vaccinations regularly? Do we follow the doctor's advice? Do we plan financially for our future? Unless we change our priorities in midlife, the perfect retirement home, the perfect children (whatever they are), will not be enjoyable if we have lost our health.

Critical-thinking fitness, or the ability to think and understand, becomes increasingly important in coping with midlife and late life changes. The intense use of the brain—our ultimate treasure—is critical at midlife. That is the time to learn or relearn a foreign language or to redirect a career. We do not want to become too content with what we have learned and achieved. Our cognitive facilities require stimulation, just as our body requires exercise. Exercise enhances cognitive abilities; both are essential. Charles Dickens wrote, "Minds, like bodies, will fall into a pimpled, ill-conditioned state from mere excess of comfort."

It is easier for the older person to solve emerging problems if a psychological repertoire has already been developed. An older adult can be imprisoned by the expectations and views of others if goals and tasks are delayed too long. A person in this time of life suffers not only from stereotypical thinking of society and the resulting prejudices, but also from environmental changes such as moving, retiring, and end-of-life issues. In a society where productivity at work is valued above everything else, a preparation for retirement is imperative, especially for those whose education does not provide good possibilities to build the coping strategies needed in late life. When one knows what to expect in the future and can prepare for it while still actively employed, the transition from active work life to retirement will be easier and later life will have fewer surprises.

Social capital increases in importance as we age. Expanding our social support, whether with family, friends, or colleagues, should gain momentum at midlife. Expanding social connections to compensate for inevitable losses should be a priority. Interaction with others and with the environment keeps us alert and involved and maximizes the time remaining to focus on what may seem to be difficult changes (such as inevitable changes in appearance and energy levels) that we cannot avoid.

Financial illiteracy and the failure to prepare for the expenses of later life can lead to serious problems. The fact that baby boomers will be supported by a smaller, younger cohort of social security contributors should alert the first wave of boomers expected in 2011 to the fact that social security changes are inevitable. No one is sure just yet what those changes will be, but the handwriting is on the wall—more seniors, more health care expenses, fewer contributing employees. When an eighty-five-year-old visited my counseling office several years ago, his tearful volley of concerns were troublesome: "I never dreamed I would live so long, and I don't have the money to go on . . . worse, is the fact that there will be nothing left for my wife to live on, if I should die first. What can I do?" We can avoid such dilemmas only through planning for a long life. This is especially important for everyone because of the huge income discrepancies that still exist between white and minority populations, as well as between the educated and the uneducated (Washington 2006).

Experts tell us that we need 70 percent of our pre-retirement income to live comfortably past age sixty. Unfortunately, for most people, it just isn't happening.

Planning and aging well may happen at different ages for different people. Professional sportsmen—football, basketball, baseball players—experience midlife earlier than others. Health professionals, professors, authors, artists, and others sometimes experience midlife much later. Regardless of when it happens, change is inevitable—it is a fundamental law of life. Accepting changes that accompany aging is a prerequisite to fulfillment. Learning to adapt to change, especially important in the pre-retirement years, prepares one for enjoying many benefits in later life.

The late Jules Willing advised that: "Nothing continues except change; nothing remains the same, nor should it." Life is a process of development, and resisting change leads to stagnation. Letting go of what used to be sets us free to continue our journey, and "to explore our inner selves and find our outer limits." Anticipation of inevitable changes avoids feelings of loss when we must turn away from completion of previous accomplishments and careers (Willing 1981, 204).

It has been scientifically documented that the more you know about aging changes, the less difficult these changes become. Author and researcher Hans Dietrich Schneider conducted a study in Zurich, Switzerland that confirmed that of the many factors that affect retirement, concrete and realistic plans are the most important. Schneider and others have shown that difficulties encountered by life transitions were attenuated when they were anticipated and preparations for them were made (Garrett 1991).

Midlife is the time to consider what we will leave behind to make the world a better place. John Gardner spoke to a crowded audience of aging specialists at a convention I attended. His openness to new ideas and different cultures, and his belief that things will always get better, gave presidents and colleagues strength. Like an aged and wise old Indian chief, his questions to his audience focused on the theme, "What have you done to make things better?" Gardner was a national treasure who served six American presidents. In spite of political ups and downs, he always remained positive, hopeful, and upbeat under difficult changing political circumstances. Gardner wrote several books, all emphasizing renewal. He promoted happiness as always learning, writing that "life is an endless unfolding, and we wish it to be an endless and unpredictable dialogue between our own potentialities and the life situations in which we find ourselves. You never conquer the mountain . . . you only conquer yourself," he stated (Gardner 1986, 4).

In a speech he defined maturity:

You learn not to engage in self-destructive behavior. You learn not to burn up energy in anxiety. You discover how to manage your tensions, if you have any, which you do. You learn that self-pity and resentment are among the most toxic of drugs. You find that the world loves talent, but pays off on character. . . . There are men and women who make the world better just by being the kind of people they are. (Gardner 1990, 4)

Midlife is the time to edit the home video, to fix up those relationships, to leave the first stage of life on which we performed, and to prepare for the second stage. We need "reserves of energy in order to plan meaningfully and creatively . . . periods of stillness can lead to invigorating times later, [but] they will not do so on their own" (Trauth and Bernstein 2007, 1). Later life guarantees that metabolism will slow down and that system changes will influence our motivation.

I did not anticipate that I would not always be able to climb a ladder to paint the white bricks on my Savannah home. One fall, fortunately without breaking a bone, provided the warning that change was necessary. Then came a root canal that my endodonist failed to correct after three different surgeries, causing much suffering. He convinced me that he would succeed the next time. I also refused to give up. Months later, still dealing with the pain, I gave in to losing the tooth. Equally foolish was wearing open-toed sandals to a funeral: I tripped and fell face down, losing my two front crowns and splitting my lower lip. And, it was my hearing loss that made me realize that I had to finish my doctoral program and take my oral doctoral examinations while I could still hear the questions asked in German. I hurriedly began to finish the required dissertation and other essential academic tasks because I could not depend on my ears to retain adequate ability to communicate.

Aging events gradually awaken us to the fact that things are changing, and adjustments are required. This realization can be the catalyst that we need to complete unfinished tasks. I remembered my last discussion with Herr Simon Decker, (my eighty-five-year-old neighbor and mentor in Germany) who, just before his death, had memorized many of Friedrich Schiller's poems. When I asked him why he had committed so many poems to memory, he explained that he was losing his vision and could no longer depend on reading his cherished book of Schiller's poems.

Without prior planning and priority adjustments, it will be more difficult to change directions at eighty than it would have been at age fifty. Otherwise, retirement may not be as easy as we had hoped. An Ameriprise Financial study in 2006 verified this uneasiness: five years after retirement 40 percent of retirees indicated unhappiness and the desire to return to work. Trauth and Bernstein also report that for those over age fifty-five, the divorce rate is now higher than at any previous time in the United States (2007).

One must be realistic about the changes and limits of later life. Only if informed about the new role that will follow, and only when one comes to grips with expected future adjustments, can one effectively cope with minimal conflict. Through preparation, one loses the dread and anxiety about aging and greatly enhances the possibility of happiness in later life (Schneider 1981).

Surveys of employees of Zurich, Switzerland confirmed that those individuals who had a positive attitude about aging and had made plans for retirement had a better adjustment. They generally felt happier and were not bored. Survey responders indicated a higher meaning in life from concrete and realistic plans (Schneider 1981).

Lowering stress is critical to good health, but without some tension between who we are and what we are becoming, we stagnate. We enjoy the freedom of midlife, but we must ask "freedom for what?" Nature has provided us with an extra gift of life in this century. We must ponder, "for what purpose?" George Bernard Shaw said that "an eternal vacation is a living hell." He implies that a vacation should be a break from something we are doing. We then return with renewed motivation and energy to whatever task stands before us. We have been re-created to meet new challenges. Midlife should re-create us to gather our reserves to do whatever we can do . . . better. As long as we deny where we are, we cannot bloom where we are planted. And remember, even if you are on the right track, if you just sit there you will get run over!

The potentials created by our new longevity can be realized only when we set aside the conventional views of aging in our society and prepare to blaze new trails as we "strike a match til time catch." These potentials will remain dormant if we do not ask ourselves, "If I don't do this, who will? If I don't do it now, then when?"

Mature, well-informed individuals must be aware that as much as 40 percent of life can transpire after retirement. The future of this long-lived generation is dependent on engagement with important roles in life that lie ahead. A lifelong continuity ensures a life cycle that the retirement years provide for a strong interaction between generations. When one is informed and prepared, many age-specific problems can be mastered and one can remain productive. The maladjustment of aging can be reduced through these ways. Without doubt, preparation leads to reduced conflicts in dealing with aging challenges. There is no way to avoid the consequences of bad habits. However, if we make the right choices, stay committed, and develop community to support our choices, the consequences will be what we desired. These can be remembered easily as the four Cs: Choices, Commitment, Community, and Consequences.

— five —

THE COPERNICAN SWITCH

"Nature appears to have focused everything on individuality,
yet makes nothing out of the individual."

Johann Wolfgang von Goethe

Although Galileo made the first complete astronomical telescope and used it to gather evidence that the earth revolved around the sun, it was Copernicus who finally published—at age seventy—these findings and discovered that the earth and those of us on the earth are really not the center of the universe. It is this similar realization—that we are not the center of the world around us—but that we are a part of all that surrounds us, that gives life meaning when we are old.

69

The goals of the individual in the first phase of life are reproduction, rearing children, and the acquisition of wealth and status. Through reproduction, an individual transcends his own limitation of life. Life continues through his seed; the reproductive cells are life itself. After the planting or joining of reproductive cells, new life is capable of further reproduction—life has been created. The individual, a beautiful expression of the thread of life, is necessary only to carry on life and, after a limited time in the stream of world events, must return to the earth. The individual's limited life is not, in itself, a goal of nature. The goal of nature is simply preservation of the form of life itself (Seitelberger 1982). Playwright Johann Wolfgang von Goethe said of nature, "Nature appears to have focused every-thing on individuality, and makes nothing out of the individual." As far as nature is concerned, individuals need only to live through the years in which they bear, and presumably care for their young. Although the human body is largely self-renewing and lasts a remarkably long time, it plays a relatively brief part in the evolution of the species (Skinner 1983, 129).

Author Avery Weisman warned, "Let us not forget that everybody is forgettable, and that even the famous will dwindle within a generation or two. When viewed against the ideal, we are all anonymous, uncelebrated, pretty shabby specimens.

There is very little that encourages much confidence in the importance of individuality" (1984, 148).

In late life many of us still believe that our focus should be on our own individual lives, as Freud promoted. Others expanded the idea. Later views have contributed to the belief that individuality is irrelevant. In fact, self-focus in late life may be the reason that some older adults see aging as an assault, or even more dreadful, as a massacre.

It is only in learning our place in nature that we can tolerate this massacre. Philosopher Joseph Fabry, author of *The Pursuit of Meaning*, wrote that we are experiencing a "Copernican switch," from the belief that man is the center of the universe, to the realization that he is but an insignificant part of the periphery (1968).

This realization is especially challenging for older men who have had control over others in the workplace, or over their spouses and children. The self-focus of many older men, and the abuse of power when tolerated, often increase in later life as other sources of strength diminish. Self-focused older adults find it very difficult to reach out to others—often alienating others and leading to self-alienation. Reaching out to others becomes increasingly important in late life in order to defocus self. However, self-preservation may become more important than any other aspect of life, even on the growth and happiness of those close to the older person. When power, once attained through work or at home, threatens self-image, anger and rage expressed to those around them is quite common. Stress is ratcheted up when aging brings less power and more idle time. Reactions in unhappy late marriages, which older adults have kept intact for one reason or another, may surface at unexpected times. Time together may allow unexpressed feelings to surface.

One retired older adult told me that when skiing with her late husband, they were caught in a descending fog on the top of the mountain. As the fog reached their level and dusk rapidly enveloped them, her husband rushed madly ahead to get to the bottom of the mountain, totally forgetting that she was there. Animal survival overtook him as the fog blinded the path downward. She was terribly frightened, but slowly descended from ten thousand feet to the bottom of the mountain. She never went skiing with him again, except in bright sunshine. She never felt totally secure from that moment forward as trust for her safety had been threatened. Self-survival as a reaction to fear had caused her husband to focus entirely on himself. Examining the transition from retirement to our final years reveals a facet of personality repressed for many years, whether in relationships to spouse, parents, or others. A reaction to aging and stress can lead to concentration on self-survival, rather than on reaching out and protecting others.

The last phase of life could provide an advance toward a new fulfillment. The true nature and best of our abilities surfaces only in old age when we are challenged with the limitation of time and the unavoidability of death. Only with the release of control at work and control of others do we make maximum use of time and abilities. This phase of life is more personal, disinterested, original, and more fully evolved. There is too little time to do much, but too much time to do little, as someone in midlife once told me.

Old age is given to man as a gift of nature, during which time we are able to expand and fulfill our accomplishments. Because of the gift of his brain, man has a special position in nature. In nature, it is only the human who is aware of the time limitations of his existence and of the finality of death. Only humans can overcome the limitations of individuality and limited existence. It is possible for everyone to become eternal because knowledge continues in those who live after him/her. The basis of the creation of the higher world of culture is found in the brain. Intellectual work can create more than life, but physical reproduction creates only life. In looking back on our lives and our mistakes and accomplishments, we are able to analyze them, to synthesize our findings, and to pass them on to the next generation. Old age is made meaningful only through intellectual or creative pursuits. The discrepancy between physical limitation and spiritual eternity challenges us to creatively overcome and accept this phenomenon of aging. In this lies the true value of aging (Seitelberger 1982).

Cognitive health is crucial to successful aging and, although the risk for cognitive decline increases with age, diseases that affect the brain are diseases—not a part of normal aging. By strengthening the health of our cognitive abilities, we are able to comprehend the human condition, to change our behavior, to bury our past hurts, and to defocus self. We are now aware that we are capable of expanding and fulfilling our accomplishments in the second half, or phase, of life.

This latter phase (change of life, or *wendepunkt*) of advancement to a higher level is, however, fraught with difficulties. Demands from within and without tax or exceed available resources of the individual, social system, and the environment. This passage from the natural or procreative phase of existence to the mature phase is a difficult and bitter process for many people. We like our comfort zones, and unless we can meet the challenges of aging and shake ourselves free from our comfort zones, we will not experience that triumphant crown of life about which the pope spoke. The later in life we try to change our behavior, the more difficult it becomes.

The challenge of adulthood is to make sense of life at a stage when changes and losses occur with bewildering and sometimes overwhelming frequency and intensity. The enormous gains in longevity, as a result of medical and technological progress, have been accompanied by widespread confusion over the meaning and purpose of late life. The older person requires a sense of meaning in his life to cope successfully with the eroding and debilitating diminishments that aging often introduces. In contrast to the findings of Sigmund Freud, man no longer suffers from sexual frustration at this period of his life, but rather from existential frustration. His main complaint is no longer a feeling of inferiority, but rather a feeling of futility, of meaninglessness and emptiness, which Frankl terms the "existential vacuum." The main complaint is boredom (Kimble and Ellor 1989).

A research project in 1988 by the Allensbacher Institute for Demographics determined that every third German complained about boredom on Sundays and holidays, in contrast to every fifth German in 1958. When asked whether they wanted to live one hundred fifty years in full control of

their strength, only 38 percent of the respondents gave a spon-
taneous "yes" in contrast to 55 percent thirty years prior. The
decreasing desire for a biblical old age was documented
through seven more questionnaires. The number of the skep-
tical grew from 11 percent in 1956 to 28 percent many decades
later (Stackelberg 1985). The problem is judging whether life
is or is not worth living. The title of Robert Butler's Pulitzer
Prize-winning book, *Why Survive?: Being Old in America*
reflects the question often asked in America, for what do we
survive? Butler states that "old age in America is often a
tragedy. We are so preoccupied with defending ourselves from
the reality of death that we ignore the fact that human beings
are alive until they are dead. At best, the living old are treated
as if they are already half dead" (Butler 1975, xi). According to
Frankl, people have enough to live by, but nothing to live for;
they have the means, but no meaning (Frankl 1984).

Everyone faces changes in old age—some are desired, some
are clearly not. Old age is merely one of a series of developmental crises that we encounter. These crises and changes
demand adjustments, including forfeiture of earlier behavior,
duties, and rights, and assumption of newer duties, jobs, and
rights. The physical, psychological, social, and legal changes
may bring demands on the person that can go beyond his or

her capacity. Development of defenses against loss, whether loss of power, job, or loved ones is common among older adults, especially among those who desire power over someone or something in order to feel valuable. Unfortunately, many lack precisely those resources that can best sustain people in crises—"mature, interpersonal relationships, a rich emotional life, and above all, spiritual community" (Ramsey 2007, 58).

Challenges increase when one realizes that the world no longer revolves around oneself, but that one is only on the periphery. Man finds identity and immortality to the extent to which he commits himself to a cause greater than himself. The more he can forget himself, giving himself to a cause to serve—or another person to love—the more he actualizes himself. Self-actualization is not an attainable goal. It is only possible as a side effect of self-transcendence. Albert Einstein said it more simply, "Only a life lived for others is worthwhile." Self-transcendence of human existence denotes the fact that being human always points to, and is directed toward, something or someone other than oneself, be it a meaning to fulfill or another human to encounter.

In late life, we are called to become more personal, more complete persons, and to face life with all of our resources. Success in late life is a matter of intelligently grasping the meaning of individual life. The success we make of retirement and post-retirement will be the test of our success in negotiating the second turning point in life, the maturity of the person. "What youth found outside and has to find, the older person should find inside. The older person has the time to get to know his internal values and to deepen them to lead a fuller life" (Tournier 1978). It is unfortunate that this realization comes so late in life that we do not always have the wherewithal to deepen those inner resources.

six

THE POWER OF PERCEPTION—ATTITUDES MATTER

"It is hard to fight an enemy who has outposts in your head."

Sally Kempton

In spite of the increasing number of older persons in our society, they still belong to a fringe group. Attitudes about aging are still tainted by minimal prestige, "social death," or the loss of meaningful human relationships—long before physical death actually occurs. As a class, old folks tend to be viewed as politically, intellectually, and economically impotent. Right or wrong, this perception limits their power and hinders their rights and possibilities. Nowhere in American society can one find a topic replete with more myths and stereotypes, and it seems to defy levels of education, geographical, and cultural differences (Tibbits 1979).

A distorted view of the abilities of older adults pervades the stereotypes. One possible explanation for this concerns the earlier norms established by psychologists for older adults' abilities. Psychologists long endorsed the centuries-old idea that intellectual and biological developments occur in parallel. Cross-sectional research on atypical older adults (surveys that questioned participants only once) further endorsed that idea. These surveys of adults were taken in nursing homes because of the convenience of large pools of older adults willing to participate. However, in those days, nursing home residents were not typical of most older adults. This negative portrayal of older adults' intellectual abilities played a large role in fostering today's subconscious behavior of older adults (Hohmeier 1978).

Integration of the elderly into society is hampered by their stereotyped medical image of being frail and demented. Stereotypes result in causing elders to behave as society expects. In spite of encouragement afforded by self-help, and despite being offered countless social programs, the elderly are still—by and large—politically controlled. The problem lies, not just with older people themselves, but with the minimalist expectations imposed upon them by the disenfranchisement of society. America's virtual image of aging is negative: the older adult is associated with isolation, dependence, and need. Research indicates that older people do not naturally turn to aberrant behaviors: it results from society's low expectations of them (Lehr 1984). Older people internalize the generally negative role that society portrays and are encouraged to retire; if they don't, they are sometimes criticized and ridiculed. My own son-in-law, whose parents retired early, cannot seem to understand why I continue to enjoy work and remain employed.

Research findings indicate that negative views of aging become self-fulfilling. The impact of expectations of physical loss leads to the belief that decline cannot be controlled and that limited future time may not allow for health improvement. Discouragement can lead to loss of immunity, and that can lead to health impairment. On the other hand, a positive view of the future, even if unrealistic, may be physiologically protective. The key to improving healthy aging is to change societal views on aging that, to a considerable extent, shapes individual views. Older persons, especially women who are poorly educated, single, and living in rural areas, are doubly disadvantaged when compared to formerly-employed, higher-educated single women living in urban areas near other women. The lower classes of older adults are further disadvantaged in that they are less likely to seek out health information or to adhere to healthy lifestyles; they avoid the expenses of doctors and the accompanying benefits associated with good health. This is just one factor that can contribute to the lower quality of life affecting these aging individuals.

The complex situation of older women is especially troublesome. There are few opportunities in society for older women when they are no longer needed for family affairs. More than men, older women are looked upon as a lower social class. Grey hair adds distinction to the older male, but for women it is viewed as a negative. There exists a fatalism in this group that hinders their future plans and damages thoughts about their own aging. This is not just the fault of society—it is also a lack of individual self-responsibility. Society must change its traditional role expectations of older persons and ratchet up expectations of responsibility while providing opportunities for growth and expression of talent.

At the end of the 1960s, earlier results of cross-sectional research on atypical older populations tested in nursing homes was challenged by K. Warner Schaie and his colleagues. New longitudinal research (testing the same respondents over several years) showed that intellectual development improves from cohort to cohort (groups aging together in time), and that decline is not necessarily a symptom of old age. Schaie found that changes in older adults are the result of individual development, and that change continues in undulating waves throughout life. Young adult's intelligence—as well as older people's intelligence—both develop in this manner. These longitudinal studies showed that many persons experienced an increase in intellectual abilities from seventy to eighty-five years of age; in contrast, some experience a decrease as early as ages twenty to thirty. The maintenance and growth of abilities depend upon the complexity of the environment—and not just on biological processes. In no way does intellectual development simply parallel the biological process (Altman 1983).

Present data suggests that we may be experiencing a shift in the cognitive health of older Americans. Because these trends in brain health are being tracked by the National Institute on Aging (NIA), we have hard data that substantiate beliefs about increased brain potential. Intellectual stereotypes are being debunked. MRIs reveal that brain activity in older adults uses both the right and left brain, and that the brain recruits other areas of the brain to fulfill its needs. This new synergy (left and right brain) translates into a new influence on the mind, for example, a growing desire and capacity that relates to the inherent potential of our species (Cohen 2005).

The Advanced Cognitive Training for Independent and Vital Elderly (ACTIVE) Study by the NIA documented improvements in memory and reasoning in a variety of older adults. This study demonstrated that diverse socioeconomic and racial populations benefit from traditional training. The oldest-old, normal elderly, and even those with cognitive impairment demonstrated positive cognitive training effects. Findings for the conservation and improvement of mental abilities were powerful and very specific. Memory and reasoning showed improvement across the board in diverse populations.

In 1998, the generation of new neurons in the brain was demonstrated in old nonhuman primates. In 1999, neurogenesis, the generation of new brain cells, was demonstrated in an old, terminal human-brain-cancer patient. Positive influences affect neurons, and it is known that aged animals, including humans living in enriched environments, have increased neurogenesis.

In the Health and Retirement Study by the National Institute on Aging, cognitive impairment was discovered to have dropped from 12.2 percent in 1993 to 8.7 percent in 2002 among people seventy years of age and older. These results support the notion of cognitive reserve, meaning that the brains of the more educated population in 2002 may be better able to sustain cognitive damage from pathology before signs of impairment occurs. The rate of cognitive impairment among those with higher levels of education was reduced for both the 1993 and the 2002 cohort.

Michael Merzinich discovered that our brain maps change, depending upon what we do over the course of our lives. He micromapped the electrical activity of neurons (brain cells) and after thousands of laborious surgeries with monkeys, discovered that plasticity—adaptability of the brain—is indisputable. It was only when he developed the cochlear implant, proving the adaptability of the auditory cortex, did scientists begin to understand that plasticity (adaptability) is a normal phenomenon and the brain maps change according to input to the brain. The brain is constantly adapting itself. The cerebral cortex is actually selectively refining its processing capacities to fit each task at hand. The brain is continuously "learning how to learn. It is more like a living creature with an appetite; one that can grow and change with proper nourishment and exercise" (Doidge 2007, 47).

It was in learning about this adaptability of the brain that I understood how I was able to master a foreign language in

85

midlife at age forty. I had mastered German sufficiently to pass the entrance test for graduate work at the University of Munich. I had always been indoctrinated with the myth that languages must be learned in the developmental stage of childhood when the native language is best mastered. However, what we later learned through micromapping of the brain was that a second language is not learned in the same part of the brain as the native language. With motivation and dedication, a foreign language can be learned by a healthy person at any stage of life (Doidge 2007).

We now know that adaptability of the brain exists from the cradle to the grave; radical improvements in cognitive functioning are possible even in the elderly. Although we lose brain tissue just as we lose muscle, at age eighty we still have a vocabulary of about ten thousand words, and we are still capable of increasing dendrites and synapses. The challenge is to intensely exercise the brain through new experiences and learning. "Merz" (the name used by colleagues of Merzenich) warns, however, that we can remap the brain for negative as well as positive experiences. These recent discoveries in neuroscience have been tested in research: two landmark studies have shown improvement in adult brain functioning. The most recent is the IMPACT study, a randomized controlled trial of a brain plasticity-based training program for age-related cognitive decline. This is the largest clinical trial ever to examine whether a specially designed, widely available cognitive training program significantly improved cognitive abilities in adults. Led by distinguished scientists from Mayo Clinic and the University of Southern California, the IMPACT study demonstrated that people can make statistically significant gains in memory and processing speed if they do the right kind of scientifically designed cognitive exercises. The Posit Science Brain Fitness Program (BFP) targets the speed and accuracy of auditory and language processes, and neuromodulatory systems associated with learning and memory. This study followed 487 healthy adults aged sixty-five and older. Results from this study demonstrated significantly superior improvements in generalized measures of memory and perception of cognitive performance in everyday life, when compared to a control group. The experimental group versus the control group showed that the brains of the users of BFP were twice as fast at taking in and processing speech. Gains reported were equivalent to ten years of memory improvement. Shopping lists without written note reminders, clearer conversations in noisy restaurants, feelings of more independence, and increased self-confidence were reported.

The IMPACT study results indicate that while "use it or lose it" is good advice, how you use it matters. The conventional approach to maintaining the brain falls short of the intensive challenges and practice that the brain needs. Effective, cognitive exercises can help adults think faster, focus better, and remember more. Whether the BFP as described by Posit is the most effective way remains to be seen. For my own personal development, foreign languages have been the challenge that I chose, and this has worked very well for me. A learned and continuously developed and practiced foreign language provides the much needed social interaction with others, while constantly challenging the brain to think outside one's native language.

There are various ways to challenge the brain and more are rapidly being developed and researched. Because the earliest age-related declines in cognition are associated with fluid intelligence such as reasoning and verbal memory, a current study (Boron et al. 2007) investigated the effects of cognitive training on inductive reasoning. Such training was found to be effective through individual and collaborative training, conducted independently of a trainer in the participant's home. This study showed again that older adults benefit from cognitive training—in this case, improving the accuracy of their inductive reasoning. This result indicates that cognitive maintenance and improvement are linked to sustained independence and to everyday problem solving. This particular study also examined the cumulative impact of chronic disease on training of cognitive ability but found "limited associations between disease and training effects" (Boron et al. 2007, 181).

Unfortunately, the image of older persons is often determined by just one characteristic, whether mental or physical. One trait may define or determine the entire ability of a person. For example, forgetfulness or an occasional senior moment leads many young people to think of older persons as frail, demented, lonely, or needy.

Many people avoid interaction with older adults because they perceive that there are fewer benefits for themselves than for the elderly. To receive more than to give may underlie the hesitation to become involved with older adults. This exchange theory leads to fewer contacts and lack of knowledge about aging. Mutual misunderstandings often lead to limited contact with children and grandchildren. Numerous studies indicate improved attitudes about aging after observations and contacts with them at early ages. Children are more likely to be receptive to aging issues, and they understand that aging has little to do with the value of a person. Many research projects have shown that increasing contact with older adults improves, and indeed, often totally changes attitudes of younger generations (Laube 1980).

My research at the University of Munich discovered this attitudinal improvement in a series of descriptions of older adults before and after exposure of students to older adults in seminars and lectures. The students in the education class attended lectures about aging. Students of social psychology had experience with older adults, as well as seminars about aging. The students in both social psychology seminars and in education lecture courses were queried about their attitudes toward older adults. They were instructed to complete partial sentences, for example: "Older people are . . . " 68 percent of the social psychology course students wrote positive words about the elderly; 32 percent expressed negative words. Thirty-four percent of the education lecture attendees finished the sentence with positive words but 66 percent listed negative words. Although students in both groups expressed negatives, those in the social psychology group expressed fewer negatives.

Results were similar when the students finished this sentence: "For old people life is . . . ." The lecture attendees listed negatives (60 percent); the social psychology seminar students, 40 percent negative. These differences may appear minor, but cultural change is always slow!

To a third sentence: "To work with or to interact with old people is . . ." social psychology participants gave positive answers 60 percent of the time; the lecture-only students responded positively with only 34 percent. No direct effort was made to influence attitudes; still, social psychology seminar participants listed a more positive opinion. Perhaps their knowledge and experience with older adults influenced their attitudes.

From 2006 through 2008, I witnessed changes of attitudes in medical students toward the elderly after they attended lectures and interactive sessions on aging and after interviewing healthy older adults. Evaluations of their experiences lead to comments such as:

- **"I no longer dread aging."**
- **"I now understand how important prevention is."**
- **"This older man was really cool!"**
- **"Aging can be a positive thing."**
- **"It was good to talk to a healthy senior citizen, rather than to those encountered in the clinics."**
- **"Caring for aging individuals does not have to be all bad."**
- **"Understanding the importance of listening changed everything."**

- "As a result of this experience, I have changed my mind about my own health and healthcare needs at age sixty-five."

These and hundreds of other comments were extremely rewarding because most health professionals view the elderly through a cultural lens based on dependence, decay, resistance, and obstinacy. Treatment of chronic disease is considered unpleasant. Such negative attitudes by professionals can change expectations of the elderly and can even lead to misdiagnosis. Health of the elderly is often viewed negatively by healthcare professionals as merely chronic cases to manage, yet all but impossible to cure. Psychiatrists often view the elderly as pathological variations of normal people. This negative view of the psychological condition of the elderly remains in today's society. Non-compliance of the elderly (for example, failure to follow instructions from their health professionals) is often the result of negative attitudes of the health professionals with whom they have been in contact. Negative attitudes of health professionals underlie the difficulty in using medical education to change student attitudes, even at the doctoral level.

Of course, attitudes of many students, doctors, and adults are influenced by the images of the elderly to whom they were exposed in their early childhood education. Young children sometimes see an older woman with a hump back as a witch. This is not surprising because many fairy tales that children hear or read are the stories of the Grimm brothers—Hansel and Gretel, Red Riding Hood, and other negative portrayals in literature. No wonder that such early impressions of older adults lead to later stereotypes. Negative characterizations of the elderly reign in public school textbooks. Generally, children believe the elderly are poor, needy, and easily rattled. Only 8 percent of older people in fourth grade books are recognized with qualities of responsibility, competence, and achievement orientation (Moramarch 1978).

The influence of the mass media has played a large role in strengthening stereotypes of the elderly. Older women are presented as technologically incompetent, indulgent in alcohol, and as having a sweet tooth. Commercials by pharmaceutical companies stress consumption of popular medical remedies and revitalization products. Public discussions of the elderly often focus on the crises of older adults, although most older adults manage everyday problems well. Local news focuses on three themes: celebrations of centenarians, available activities for older adults, and older adults' financial emergencies. Especially around holidays, help for needy and lonesome older adults are common requests. Of course, there are positive as well as negative aspects of these cries for public involvement.

In an analysis of commercials targeting older adults, 90 percent were related to pharmaceutical needs, especially to those remedies professed effective for many aches and pains. Jokes directed toward older adults also strengthen negative stereotypes. Two hundred and fifty jokes were analyzed by Tews, who found that over half of them presented a negative image of the elderly. For example, a female friend had been propositioned for marriage after a lovely dinner and conversation with her chaperone, an elderly man of advanced age. The morning after their evening together, she received a call from the very embarrassed man who said, "I asked you to marry me last night and I am so sorry that I have forgotten your answer." She responded, "That is quite alright because I remembered the question this morning, but could not remember who had asked me!"

Employment for older adults is difficult to obtain, especially in larger companies. Fifty percent of employers admit that they prefer younger employees. In spite of older adults' capabilities, employers still admit discriminating against them. Disadvantages are especially seen when downsizing or expansion occurs. Less attractive opportunities discourage older adults, and withdrawal from work is often the result. When describing themselves, older employees exhibit a reduced evaluation, displaying a self-fulfilling prophecy which effectively leads to less productivity. Health problems often lead to early retirement from work. It is, however, difficult to establish a direct correlation between loss of performance caused by deteriorating health, and loss caused by long-lasting stress and strain in the workplace (Tews 1979). Some experts say that it is only above age seventy-five that health really becomes a dominant consideration in the work place. Obviously, there are exceptions like Claude Pepper and Strom Thurmond, who remained active in politics in their ninth decades.

This negative picture of aging could result from anxiety about death. Europeans complain that Americans exhibit horror and fear of corpses, funerals, and burials; we try not to identify with death. The embalming and expensive clothes in which to be buried are attempts to cover the deteriorating body. The Germans simply close the wooden box container at death and leave pictures of the person for family and friends. When I attended a friend's funeral in Munich, this seemed to be a much more sensible and natural approach. When my trusted mentor, Herr Decker, died, his former students, church staff, family, and friends gathered around his grave and testified to the good memories of times past with the deceased. As we sprinkled water on his wooden box in the earth, we chanted refrains. Then lunch and fellowship celebrated the life of our deceased and beloved friend.

I witnessed very negative feelings about the elderly in Germany. Many young people still blame older adults for Hitler's success. Very few young people understand that it was those same adults who bore the burden of rebuilding Germany after the war, removing the rubble, and leading the reconstruction. They simply asked the elderly, "How could you have let this happen?" They could not understand how the elderly dealt with the past, probably a basic reason for much misunderstanding between generations everywhere (Borchert and Derichs-Kunstmann 1982). Of course, prejudice against Jewish people or against minorities in other countries is equally damaging. Yet, each culture and ethnic group has strengths that are needed in society.

All stereotypes are based in the core values of societies. When the elderly are housed on the edge of town in nursing homes, they lose economic independence, autonomy, personal and career identities, spouses, children, and familiar acquaintances. When they enter a nursing home, their lives are controlled by others. This increases social isolation, decline, and psychological self-worth. The lack of bargaining power is the result of the cumulative effects of losses (Dye 1980).

Older people find themselves in an ambivalent situation. On the one hand, they are declassified and discouraged; on the other hand, they are seen as wise and blessed with a lifetime of experience. Many adults over age seventy are active and productive; they often become wiser and more insightful with increasing age. Yet, stereotypes are based on the sick and needy. Older people must advocate that their image of helplessness is incorrect, and that the last phases of life remain challenging but positive.

Because all matter is interconnected, it is clear that interdependence is mandatory for survival. Using the image of letting go found in Hindu philosophy, Erik Erikson described a mother cat picking up a kitten in her mouth, the kitten completely relaxed, hanging limp and infinitely trusting in its maternal benevolence. The kitten responded instinctively, but we humans require a whole lifetime of practice to do this (Erikson 1986). Society will evolve fruitfully only if we are prepared to trust those younger than ourselves and to hand over the leadership to them. It is not necessary to continue to give orders to find meaning in life. One must relinquish authority and not hang on to a secret nostalgia for the previous life, its joys and sorrows, its victories and struggles, and the social status it conferred. Otherwise, the older person is not free enough in her mind to construct a new future. Just as in driving a car, one cannot engage a new gear without first disengaging the old, so a real detachment from the past is a condition for a fruitful present (Frankl 1984).

Because of the power of perception, it is critical that we showcase older adults who defy stereotypes. Changing the images of aging is slowly occurring. For example, I remember Marie, a friend from the Senior Friendship Days program in Palo Alto, California. Marie appeared every Thursday with a basket full of succulents that she had rooted for members of her gardening group. Tireless in her dedication to her "students," she never faltered in holding their interest. Unforgettable was the day in 1989 when an earthquake hit San Francisco. Everyone but Marie scurried out of the Palo Alto Community Center where the program was in progress. I was terrified by the noise of the rumbling earth and the chaos created by hundreds of seniors scattering hurriedly to get outside. Not exactly the brave leader, I followed them outside to witness trees swaying back and forth, and yellow tree pollen filling the air. My fear overcame me as I cried out, "I cannot die; I have not finished my dissertation." That was the levity that everyone needed as they laughed at what seemed very trivial in the face of a natural disaster. We waited outside until the earth calmed. When we reentered the building, Marie was sitting calmly under the scaffolding at the entrance. When queried why she had stayed indoors and had faced possible collapse of the building, her comment was: "My husband, who engineered the San Francisco bridge, designed this building, and I knew it would not collapse."

This amazing woman, at ninety-three, when asked whether she ever became fatigued, answered, "Yes, I do, and when I do, I get on the floor and do a hundred sit-ups!"

Another example defying the negative stereotypes of aging was Patricia, an African American nurse, who, at age 76, reentered the work force through affiliation with the Center on Aging. She was the first African American to receive the doctor of philosophy from Vanderbilt University. She was the most reliable employee for the decade that I directed the Aging Consortium for Meharry, Vanderbilt, and Tennessee State University. When our funding expired and I could not keep her on staff, she returned to Tennessee State University (TSU) as interim dean of the School of Nursing. Acquaintance with Patricia was a learning experience. Often observing my impatience at getting things accomplished in the university environment as quickly as I wished, she would say, "Ruth, you have returned to the South, where some cultures just move slower!"

All bureaucracies have difficult and slow processing systems. I learned that first at the University of Georgia and again at the University of Munich, where things that I could accomplish in a day in Nashville would take a week or longer in Munich. Acquiring copies of journal articles, books, and recent information about aging would take so long that I would contact the dean at Armstrong Atlantic University in Savannah, Georgia, to order copies from their system and mail them to me in Munich. By the time I had received the articles from Georgia and had written a chapter in German, the articles with the same information in German would arrive from the archives of the University of Munich's library, giving me the German data references for my dissertation.

Mature adults can resolve dilemmas with more ease and confidence than they could have earlier in life. They also do this with a light heart and a sense of humor. Marie and Patricia confirmed what I had already learned: maturity brings the wisdom needed to cope with inevitable changes and challenges of aging. Their examples and those of many others can change perceptions of the elderly. Although we have few successfully retired role models who use their time as their ally instead of their enemy, more are developing second careers and finding meaning through community and caring. We must increase the number of role models to whom we can relate.

seven

NARCISSISTIC INJURY AND LOSS

"we delight in the beauty of the butterfly, but rarely admit the changes it has gone through to achieve that beauty."

Maya Angelou

Narcissistic injury is the greatest problem of aging. The exaggerated self-love associated with the legend of Narcissus, who fell in love with his own image, is not meant here. Narcissism refers to the person's basic self-concept, the central ego-unifying image of self. The mastery of skills and acquisition of powers, painfully acquired throughout life, wane in the last phase of life. One's resources, energies, adaptability, and functionality—and the intimacies of relationships upon which one depended are continually being depleted and lost (Bianchi 1982).

The elderly are faced with lack of role clarity. There are fewer and fewer clear-cut obligations of appropriate behavior as one passes into old age. Therefore, there is little motivation to become old, and no real basis for judging success or failure in being an older person. The individual's level of uncertainty of what constitutes proper action or belief is sometimes referred to as "anomie." This state of normlessness—or lack of regulative forces within society—affects the decision-making processes and behavior of its members. In the absence of rules or restraints, man tends to strive toward indefinite goals, unable to recognize his legitimate needs or to determine the direction in which his efforts should be invested. This condition of normlessness is derived from the social or cultural structure.

No instinct tells man what he has to do, and sometimes he does not even know what he wishes to do. He either wishes to do what other people do (conformism), or he does what other people wish him to do (totalitarianism) (Frankl 1984).

Bewilderment, anxiety, lack of confidence, defensiveness, hostility, inflexibility, and decreased cognitive capacity are also associated with this state of normalness. Reduced or impaired action with others may result in mental distress. Absence of reference groups or lack of appropriate normative information cause the elderly to internalize their feelings of incompetence. This may affect their participation in social roles, their ability to adapt to environmental demands, and their felt capacity to influence, control, or master their environment. This may indicate awareness of the impossibility of achieving life's goals. A state of incongruity between a person's aims and socially-institutionalized opportunities to achieve these aims can lead to personal disorganization (Birren and Renner 1980).

Those aged persons who have had the highest degree of investments in the norms and values of their societies may experience acute social and psychological disenfranchisement. Negativism and labeling in the social organization interact with certain role loss. For persons who have always been dominant forces and providers, accepting limitations and dependency can prove difficult for themselves and for their families. There may be a secondary loss of competence in an independent elderly person from loss of pride, dignity, and even identity.

Loss of control harms the individual's well-being. Old people who maintain a feeling of control and mastery of their environment are much more able to deal successfully with the stresses of old age.

People who feel hopeless and helpless are least able to deal with stress. The losses of aging may be mainly external, but they are internalized and diminish self-image. Knowledge that human beings can transform something ugly into positive learning can help maintain stability when an older person is threatened. Unfortunately, this knowledge, though apparently adequate motivation for some, is not by itself always adequate to initiate such transformation . . . as shown in Phillip Roth's example of *Everyman* (2007). Roth's protagonist experienced, through his brother, the discipline and knowledge to transform his weaknesses into strengths, but this did not motivate him sufficiently to change his destructive behavior. When exploring the health condition of many older Americans, who are almost daily exposed to the importance of exercise, the majority of Americans over age 65 do not exercise adequately for health maintenance. Good examples of fit aging adults and the encouragement from their environment may be more influential in changing their health behavior.

Economics often threaten independence. Without sufficient income to take care of needs and pleasures, life is very difficult for the aged. Many retired people receive a total pension income from public and private sources of one-half or less of their average pre-retirement income. Without raising the question of the adequacy of retirement incomes, a 50 percent reduction in anyone's income is highly likely to produce stress. Widows, single women, and members of minority groups are particularly economically disadvantaged. Many older women are society's poorest. Being poor would have a different meaning, and poverty would be less terrifying, if older people were assured essential public and social services such as transportation, adequate medical care, decent public housing, and rent subsidies. However, in America such essential services are not always available. Although commonplace in Western Europe for decades, in America universal government-backed medical insurance and public housing are still controversial and poorly implemented concepts. The socialized medicine system that exists in Europe seems, in many ways, more democratic than the American system. In Germany, for example, national assistance is granted to everyone who is unable by any other means to meet living costs, along with other specific and acknowledged needs (material and non-material). It is a last resort for all citizens, however. The origin of the national assistance program is in welfare, and many older adults find the status as a recipient of national assistance discriminatory. They often do not claim it, even when so entitled. There is much poverty among old people in other areas of Europe also.

Approximately one million older persons have an income that is the same as those receiving national assistance (Bujard 1982). However, as in America, an adequate-to-good standard of old age income is, as a rule, only attained in some European systems by pension entitlement accumulated over a normal working life without massive disruptions, and under full utilization of insurance possibilities. In Europe, as in America, for many widows who have not experienced a career in gainful employment of their own, the pension payment is little more than exercise of a social welfare obligation.

Reforms in social security and pension plans have been a boost to many Americans. However, very recent changes in retiree health and pension plans have placed their future in jeopardy. There are still millions of poor and near-poor elderly people. The economic downturn during the late 2000s has left many older adults with limited choice, as well as reduced pension funds. The two-trillion-dollar loss in retirement funds severely affects older adults, many of whom will not live long enough to experience the turn around in our economy. Also, because many older adults depend on the equity in their homes to buy into a retirement facility or assisted living, hardship results for those who cannot sell their homes during the housing crisis. So, in spite of social security benefits, pensions, and Medicare, all the benefits that offered elders status, and even fringe roles as financially productive workers, have been lost by recent changes created by the economic crisis. Unemployment rates are rising in America, and just as during the Industrial Revolution, older people are the last to be hired and the first to be fired. The number of unemployed workers seventy-five and older is up 46 percent from January 2008, with the jobless rate of those over sixty-five at 5.7 percent. However, the increase in the work force among people seventy-five and older has recently risen from 4.7 percent to 7.3 percent. In the present recession, many older adults are even looking for minimum wage jobs (Ansberry 2009).

Medical costs of all kinds have risen so much that they are beyond the reach of a large segment of the population. Individuals eighty-five and over are especially hard hit, particularly those not living in family units. They are, on average, poorer than individuals sixty-five to seventy-four years of age. Also, these economic problems are especially acute for minorities. The 12 percent of white older Americans whose income falls below the federal government's poverty line compares with 22 percent of Hispanic elderly, 32 percent of Native American elderly, and 35 percent of black elderly.

There really is no simple solution for such economic problems, but possibilities include new insurance policies, a reverse mortgage possibility for home owners, diversification of present investments, and, as a last resort, help from their very capable children. I have become aware of the urgent need to teach young adults the importance of investing early and systematically, and of home ownership. For young and old, having to meet monthly mortgage payments can cut down on discretionary spending. Otherwise, monthly rental payments can consume a major portion of income, especially of a retiree's fixed income.

When aging brings with it the necessity to change living situations, independence may be sacrificed. Fear of loss of independence is why so many old people stubbornly refuse to be transferred to an institution of any kind. These homes are often seen as the last station of life and are therefore avoided at all costs by older adults. Living in an institution often promotes dependence on organizational rituals, restricts autonomy, and limits personal choices. Institutional living sometimes seems to encourage an early resignation from society, a removal of certain participation in the outside community and, consequently, a segregation of the aged. The process of moving into a retirement home does not solve all problems of aging. It improves the packaging—promising dances, arts, crafts, and other attractions. It is a solution without substance, and underlies a poverty of imagination. When one moves into a smaller accommodation, or into a retirement home, or loses neighbors and a familiar environment, the question of the meaning of life surfaces (Curtin 1972).

The popular saying, "one shouldn't transfer old trees" is not always true, however. Moving is not always damaging, especially if the older person voluntarily moves and can adjust and master the new situation. Many residents of retirement homes become actively involved in the world of the institution after having disengaged from life on the outside. Being with others, engagement in the social world of the institution that stands outside the larger world appears to foster some opportunities for autonomy with a structure of dependence (Pastolon 1981).

However, moving to any new residence can profoundly affect the way the person feels. Change can affect relationships in the present environment, physical and emotional well-being, and can lead to helplessness, feelings of anxiety, depression, despondency, and sadness. This may explain why the majority of older people are determined to live as independently as possible for as long as possible. Living in one's home and owning a house are important goals that are often based on individuality and independence. Once home owner-ship is attained, it is usually relinquished only under stressful circumstances in old age. The reduction of demands in late life is not always desirable. Expectations from the environ-ment in the form of mild demands are important, and the environment should demand more from many old people than is accepted by them.

Families do not necessarily live in a house together, but they remain critical to aging persons. Families are a major source of socialization in late life, whether through children, grandchildren, or other relatives. Family relationships have a widely influential subconscious dynamic—there are inter-changeable dependencies, emotional and material bindings, and controversial meaning and valuing of the connections. Most older persons clearly wish to maintain relationships with their children throughout life. The attachment to the parent does not end in late childhood or adolescence, but persists throughout the lifespan. The propensity for closeness and contacts continues. Although the myth continues that old people are alienated from their children, and the subject has guided much research for the past thirty years, data indicate that most children are not alienated from their older parents.

In any relationship there is ambivalence, especially where emotions are strong and feelings of duty and nearness are predominant, even when potential for alienation is strong. Research bears out the folk wisdom: there seems to be new rapport and empathy between parents and children once the children become parents themselves. Daughters especially experience a renewed closeness to their own mothers when they themselves become mothers (Fisher 1986).

Although urbanization and job mobility have challenged kinship bonds in contemporary society, a modified extended family still seems to exist. Viable relationships are typically maintained, despite the physical separation of older persons from their relatives. Family relationships may have gained momentum because of weakening ties between family and community. Freedom from economic interdependency may have led to more voluntary family ties. However, kinship relationships are merely a latent potential from which active and viable relationships may or may not develop (Pifer 1986).

Although it is relatively seldom that parents live under the same roof with their children, it is because the majority of old people choose to live apart from their children. The unwillingness of children to live with their parents should not be seen as negative. Distance is a type of protection that may help all involved. Relationships may weaken as the child grows and establishes appropriate peer relationships that promote independence. This has been described as intimacy at a distance, and suggests that geographical distance does not necessarily mean cooler relationships. It means simply that in the media and in today's information society that has replaced earlier traditions, each person needs space to reflect and to become aware of one's own needs and identity (Rosenmayr and Rosenmayr 1983).

There are, however, many elderly adults without children. Friendship is important for all adults but it is critical for those without close family members. Dante said, "Without friendships is life's enjoyment greatly lacking." In nature one always has a friend, in books many, and still more in caring for and sharing with others. Cicero wrote that life cannot be worth living if it does not repose on the mutual goodwill of a friend. He writes:

What is sweeter than to have someone with whom you may dare discuss anything as if you were communing with yourself? How could your enjoyment of prosperity be so great if you did not have someone whose joy in them would be equal to your own? Adversity would indeed be hard to bear, without him to whom the burden would be heavier even than to yourself. (1979, 131)

I attended an international meeting of aging professionals and listened intently to speakers from many foreign countries discuss how extended families cared for their elderly, and how they had provided supplementary services in the community as needed. Another eureka moment struck me! We must develop extended neighborhoods in America, because extended family extends from Boston to San Francisco. Bonding neighborhoods into community support systems would not only provide the friendship that older adults need, but could possibly provide informal care for each other. Planning ahead is incomplete when one fails to consider the probability that one's capacities will decline. From that experience forward, I began to investigate successful programs that keep older adults in their homes.

The "Aging in Place" initiatives in America have led some extended neighborhoods to replace previous family care for the elderly with help from extended groups of older adults. These initiatives begin in each member's current neighborhood, but subsequent residences may be appropriate to changing personal situations, including shared housing and continuing care retirement communities. Although Aging in Place has been initiated in many places, Aging in Community is more descriptive of the plans that I envision.

Because our society finds many elderly persons far removed from their natural families, innovations to bind communities together through programs such as Community Without Walls appear to improve the quality of life for older adults. This concept brings together service agencies, volunteers, businesses, and civic groups to create a network that addresses seniors' health, social needs, and isolation. With an outlook toward the future, mobilization of resources can accomplish a higher quality and more productive life. We must continue to create something new, because old solutions do not solve today's challenges. Destiny begins with a new vision.

My vision is that the creativity, abilities, and wisdom of older adults will lead to the unfolding of their full potential. The energy of many older adults, who want to meet their own needs for as long as possible as they age, can be tapped. I believe this to be possible without accepting a mortgage on the future. It requires that we unite to maintain abilities, to understand the connections linking mental, physical, and emotional qualities, and the rewards of a continuous involvement in the lives of others. Sharing resources can be a significant factor toward a more meaningful life. Socialization within a neighborhood is increasingly important as siblings and friends leave through illness and death, or because of career changes. Maintaining control, making decisions, directing one's own schedule, and continuing to be responsible for basic needs can enhance and improve quality of life.

The financial resources of older adults are also more under their control when they live in their own neighborhood. When crunching the numbers, I discovered that a senior living at home can live an additional year for approximately $15,000. In an assisted living facility, this cost rises to $50–$70,000 (or much more, depending on health conditions). That cost approaches a million dollars in a decade. Living in a nursing home at the taxpayer's expense, a decade of life can cost even more than a million dollars. Planning for a longer life requires allocating financial resources prudently to stretch them for decades. We must take the lead as we enter this stage of life in which financial expenditures must be prudently controlled.

The Beacon Hill Boston Model is one of the oldest, most successful programs designed to keep seniors in their homes. I ordered their manuals and videos and talked with their director. I engaged former student Steve Mathews (retiree and widely known advocate for older adults) to help me investigate and plan; we met regularly for several months. I visited the

Beacon Hill program, the Avenidas Aging in Place program in Palo Alto, California, and the Princeton Community Without Walls program. As I continued to investigate programs developing nationally, Aaron Brill, MD (a professor at Vanderbilt University), Steve, and I decided to create a pilot of the Princeton model of Aging in Place program. We called it Community Without Walls. We approached Temple Hills Golf Club to arrange use of their club house for a site to hold monthly meetings.

From Temple Hills, the former president of their home-owner's association sent surveys to members of the community; some were returned. Interest in learning about a Community Without Walls neighborhood program was weak, yet sufficient to gather a group large enough to qualify as the first house. Following the Princeton model, we wanted to develop small groups (called houses, chapters, or sub-groups) of members living in proximity to one other.

By January 2008, attendance was large enough to designate House One (or Chapter One) as a development pointed in the right direction. With the goal of empowering seniors to use their own skills, to get to know their neighbors, and to be adequately informed to make choices that would permit them to age in place (in their communities), we created interest for the program. Our goal was to strengthen bonds among community members to help each other with simple tasks.

The pilot community rose to the occasion. Volunteers staffed the program, including professors from Vanderbilt and Meharry Medical colleges (Brill and Garrett), the president-elect of the Council on Aging (Steve Mathews), and local residents who contributed greatly by connecting people through email and phone calls about notices of meetings. A thriving community of seniors helping seniors began to evolve, with a projected token fee for membership to finance structuring a non-profit business model. Mathews secured a charter and a business identification number from the state of Tennessee in 2009, grant proposals were submitted, and more volunteers are still being recruited today. Our official opening of the program was held in May 2009, with speaker Walter Bortz, MD, a well-known professor from Stanford University and author of several books about aging.

Meantime, as I attended successful programs, I continued to meet with their officers and compare program goals, costs, and developments. I also began to study other cultures' solutions. For example, the Japanese take every opportunity to learn about the needs of older adults. I had spoken to the Japanese ministerium a decade ago about programs for the elderly. I discovered a culture seriously committed to responsibility for elder care. Faced with rapidly aging populations and serious concerns of an increasing caregiver burden, the Japanese have committed themselves to universal and equitable access to long-term care, regardless of socioeconomic status or family availability.

The Chinese culture has interested me for many years because of their taxation of couples who bore more than one child. This was a short-sighted political strategy to limit the size of families. Thirty years after the one-child policy of family planning was implemented, the problem of how to care for two sets of aging parents has become a pressing concern for one-child couples. Their past model of family responsibility for their elders is no longer appropriate for the present aging population. The highest levels of the Chinese government are therefore proposing an Aging in Place model very similar to the Community Without Walls program. With an expectation of 437 million elderly in the year 2051, the government has stepped in to address the problem. Because of a strong sense of family and belonging, approximately 85 percent of their elderly depend on family support and care. However, at present, "Traditions of raising sons for support in one's old age no longer applies and traditional patterns are close to collapse," reports

Zhou Li Juan in *Aging Today* (Wang 2008, 8). An Aging in Place program would alleviate some of the pressure on families by providing a range of support services within the community.

Although the Chinese level of governmental involvement is unlikely to be available to mainstream Americans, the home-and-community-based care in many states does indeed help many elderly remain in their homes. Unfortunately for many seniors, their income levels to qualify for these services are above the ceilings that specify income limits to receive such services. Many of these middle-income older adults do not have the finances needed to live in a retirement home for a decade or longer. However, for those who do qualify financially, empirical evidence shows that state of Tennessee Home and Community Based Service (HCBS) support may prevent or delay nursing home admission for those with limited family caregiving and financial resources. This support, which will delay or prevent nursing home admission for Medicaid-qualifying seniors, should favorably impact the state budget.

Like America, Chinese efforts to initiate such programs are faced with problems of limited trained staff and service providers. Vocational and technical training to establish universal standards for skills and services is needed. Caregivers and service providers are, in general, poorly compensated and funding for such services is limited. However, a step in the right direction has been made. This burgeoning population needs government, community, and family support. Unprecedented challenges in implementing such an initiative require a multidisciplinary approach in China, Japan, and the United States. The decrease in the number of children born to women and the increase in labor participation among women lead to a genuine concern that the caregiving burden on adult children will grow (US Bureau 2005).

The ultimate loss challenging the older person is death (Birren 1986). Although our acquaintance with loss and death spans a lifetime, and partial loss throughout our lives prepares us for the death of close family members, a lifetime of preparation cannot blunt the pain of grief, the initial shock followed by yearning, and the later waves of sadness aroused by memories of loved ones. It is natural for psychologically healthy humans to form close relationships and to suffer their loss when ties are destroyed through death or divorce.

Loss of ties to the divorcee is usually preceded by give and take. The widow, on the other hand, has little control over events. For many, if not most of the widows and widowers, death of their partners has meant not only grief associated with loss—but emotional, social, and financial problems as well. Death of a spouse interrupts those aspects of life in which the spouse has been involved as companion, resource and object of love, and the person around whom time and work were organized.

Especially for many older women in the present cohort, the spouse has often been the major source of identity. Widows must forge an uncoupled identity (Moos and Schaefer 1986). The disparity between the number of widows and widowers—caused by the longer lifespans of women and the tendency for husbands to be older than their wives—means that many widows will not remarry. Many older adults will confront widowhood, a challenging life transition that requires greater emotional, psychological, and behavioral adjustment than almost all other major life events (Wu and Schimmele 2007). Disruption by death of such social and personal losses can result in feelings of desertion, desolation, loneliness, and some-times of rejection. Contentment in old age is difficult without a confidant.

However, even among the coupled, uncoupling through divorce in late life is a new phenomenon. Wu (Wu and Schimmele 2007) reports an increasing late life divorce rate. Dissolving a troubled marriage, even in very late life, may be motivated by unfulfilled marriages resulting from increased longer lives and "developmental issues associated with personal growth in old age" (2007, 41). Because of longer lives, spouses often change and outgrow their mates. Margaret Mead explained away her three marriages by saying that none of them failed. She simply had gone through several distinct adult stages. During each stage she had become, in essence, a different person with a new and different assortment of lifestyle preferences. She discovered that she had an entirely different set of needs and priorities for a companion. When she was young, she needed a husband who could share her vigor and enthusiasm and the task of raising children. In middle age, at the height of her career as a world-famous anthropologist, she found that her parenting-oriented partner no longer fit. She was fortunate enough to find a perfect mate who could share with her the more mature intimacies of an intellectual companion and traveling partner. In her later years, as her interests turned away from the activities of the world and more inward toward spiritual concerns, she needed and found a spiritual confidant and soul mate (Roth 2007).

When life expectancy was short, we barely had time to live one adult role with one compatible mate. Now we have the time and resources to be many different people in one lifetime. Earlier, death often intervened before a typical marriage had run its natural course. Now when a typical marriage runs out of steam, the thought of twenty, thirty, or even fifty more years in an unsatisfying relationship can cause action at any age (Dychtwald and Flower 1989). As the Mead example suggests, divorce and remarriage are less an admission of failure than a shedding of skin, a breaking of a chrysalis, a moving on to the next stage. Giving up on a marriage is very different from giving up on marriage. However, according to Bruno Hamann, the increasing divorce rate and the distancing of the generations are serious problems (1988). Old age could offer couples the opportunity to move marriage from a merely functional relationship to a deeper level of love and commitment. Through the struggles of the later years, when both partners experientially know the shortness of life, a deeper devotion and intercommunion could be realized. Anne Lindbergh described an ideal couple as two sea shells no longer facing each other, but rather linked together facing outward toward the world (Bianchi 1982). Enrichment of relations within couples might be achieved by couple transcendence—couples forgetting their own individual indulgence, and instead reaching out to the community, building caring networks, and committing themselves to important causes—which could lower the divorce rate among the middle-aged and older populations.

Augustine understood that the mutual love of partners could shine more brilliantly at that time of life. He said, "But now in good, although aged, marriages, albeit there hath withered away the glow of full age between male and female, yet there lives in full vigor the order of charity between husband and wife."

However, Wu reports that few divorced older adults regret their uncoupling. Stigma of divorce has dwindled and a sense of relief from leaving a bad marriage is often reported. Personal freedom and an uncoupled identity, though often initially fraught with difficult adjustments, outweigh avoiding interaction with, or caring for, an unpleasant or unloved spouse. Whether through widowhood or divorce, financial and social support are issues often faced in postmarital transitions (Wu and Schimmele 2007).

The changing time perspective is the most conspicuous feature of aging. Many feel like life has run out; others depend on an unshakable belief in life after death. The time for concluding unfinished business becomes highly circumscribed. Difficult questions arise as the shortness of time in the face of the uncertainties of late life is pondered (Bianchi 1982). The loss of control of one's own time is often a source of conflict in intergenerational relationships. New research shows that many older couples enjoy the empty nest. Freedom from responsibilities of parenting and functioning as exemplary role models is relished. Older couples are no longer content to altruistically live their lives for their children or grandchildren. Concentration on self has filtered up (many older adults focus on their own needs, not on the needs of the generations that follow), and elders wish to live for their own fulfillment. With homes in many cases paid for and children away from home, many over the age of sixty feel entitled to a little self-indulgence; some now have sufficient discretionary incomes to act on these wishes. Reluctance to be constrained by other people's demands and concerns with aging issues and death preoccupy many aged persons. These internal concerns take energy and time and can make external demands seem particularly burdensome. Time and quiet belong to growing old.

When society and family shun and segregate the elderly, they strengthen an older person's fears of helplessness and uselessness, thereby reinforcing existing fears. If also deprived of personal control of their lives, the will to live may be eroded. The elderly are less likely to seek help for anything other than physical problems. In addition, they are less likely to seek opportunities to form new attachments that seem to require more and more energy (Schneider 1981).

Loss of a sense of belonging, previously shared with others in the work force, can cause persons to feel excluded, bereft, outside, and disposable. Previous organizations that provided goals and tasks made achievement possible. Reduction of household tasks and loss of routine from stabilizing forces of a set schedule lead many older people into dangerous wastelands of empty time. The aged become strangers in a society that is both theirs and of their making. Boredom and apathy lead to psychological, if not physical deterioration (Moos and Schaefer 1986). According to a famous French physician, people can indeed die of boredom. Or, as shown by the protagonist in *Everyman* (Roth 2007), people can think they are dying of pain, when they are really dying of envy of the success of others.

Loss of a driver's license signals the loss of freedom of independence to drive wherever and whenever a person desires. Difficulties in using public transportation cause the world of older persons to gradually shrink to include just the town, then only the neighborhood, then the house, and finally perhaps only their room. This loss of independence is sometimes accompanied by a new sense of loneliness as old people become separated from previously-treasured people and things, through failing vision and hearing, death of friends, dispersal of family, and loss of mental abilities. Health problems can severely limit activity and mobility (Tombs 1984).

In previous decades, there were many studies defining areas of life's conflicts. The following conflict areas were taken from 2,326 cases: conflicts with one's own parents and children; conflicts with relatives and in other social areas; conflicts connected with the selection of spouses; conflicts with partner relationships; with the selection of a profession; within the work area; with one's own personality; and in political situations, religious areas, and schools. The various age groups showed the following picture: conflict situations mentioned had often existed for decades. An increase in the number of conflict situations is not a special sign of advanced age, but an indication of unresolved problems. Conflicts and difficulties are not dependent upon chronological age (Lehr 1984).

In a detailed analysis of 326 autobiographies of men and women, a surprisingly large number experienced difficult situations in their relationships with their own parents. Gender differences were minimal. In all age groups, these difficulties with parents took first place with the women; with the men, difficulties with parents took second place, with work-related difficulties taking first place (Thomae 1983).

The tense situation that results from living together with parents is mentioned most often as a cause of stress. Problems develop because of certain demands by the parents and from the children's consideration of duty to the parents. The children have difficulties making their lives compatible with those of their parents. Arguments, often intense, accompany the disagreements. Conflicts with other relatives are also a problem. Often there are arguments with siblings or relatives of the spouse, and typically in advanced age, there can be problems with inheritance. There are many problems in the other social areas. Friends and acquaintances are also not exempt from complicated encounters.

There are also certain disturbing age-related factors in the workplace. They are mostly situation specific, time specific, and dependent upon certain personality structures and biographical factors. As one ages, the lack of opportunity to change career positions can be a problem. Competition with younger colleagues can occur; they are often envied because of their knowledge and youthful appearance. Such tension makes the social atmosphere for older people more difficult. Problems in the intimate aspects of life can also show up in the workplace. And, psychologically, it has been found that the patronizing attitude of supervisors replaces the advice and help that were earlier experienced. Also, just thinking about the finality of one's occupation and the decreasing chances of changing jobs can cause diminished belief in one's own ability to adjust and change (Lehr 1984).

Performance deficits can lead to problems at the place of employment or put one at risk in the labor market. The degree of relevance of these risks is determined by vocational status, the demand of the particular job, and the demand for labor in general. Some groups of workers who are beyond the normal risks of the older worker include permanent civil servants and some salaried employees in public service. Because health deterioration usually shows up in more advanced years, it is difficult to establish a direct correlation between loss of performance from deteriorating health verses long-lasting stress and strain in the workplace. In fit aging individuals it is only above age seventy-five that health really becomes a dominant consideration in the work place. Obviously, there are exceptions. Claude Pepper served as a congressman until his death at age eighty-eight. Also, Viktor Frankl was still on the lecture circuit at age eighty-four.

According to cultural observer and author Gail Sheehy, psychoanalysts and social scientists who have represented aging as synonymous with loss have drawn their conclusions from a severely limited group—from women who came to them with their anger disguised as depression, from men who brought psychosomatic complaints to cover impotence, and from people in mental hospitals and on relief rolls, in hospitals, and in homes for the aged. These people were more likely to have suffered many losses. However, contrary to impressions received by many social scientists that age is a time of depression, poor health, rejection by children, creeping impoverishment, loneliness, and loss—only approximately 5 percent of all people over age sixty-five are in institutions. The remainder are relatively independent, but the number needing help with activities of daily living (ADLs) increases after age eighty. Many of them have children living nearby, and two-thirds live in their own paid-for homes as long as possible (Sheehy 1976).

Research confirms a changing picture of the aged. A Los Angeles Times poll interviewed 3,050 adult Americans, including an over sample of middle-aged and elderly people, to provide greater statistical precision on the opinions of the older persons. By a variety of measures, the poll found that older Americans are significantly happier—or at least have less to worry about—than those who are younger or middle-aged. Fewer seniors say they are lonelier than younger people, less likely to think about death or to be afraid of it than are younger people. They have fewer financial worries. Pollster Ivan Lewis explains that this may suggest that the older one becomes, the less one needs or cares so much about material things, and that our system of caring for the elderly is working (1989). This may be a general commentary about changes in American life, but perhaps before the recent financial crisis.

Professor of Psychology Susan Krauss Whitbourne (University of Mass.-Amhurst) also reports that the negative impact of events in the lives of older people may be exaggerated. The effects of events such as children moving out or back in, death of significant others, illness, and socioeconomic status vary according to the individual's age and sex. The majority of older people experience the last phase of life as positive, except when a difficult illness takes over. She attributes this happiness to the learned ability to be able to find the best possible solutions to problems, and to be able to compromise (1985).

All of us are involved throughout life with losses of significant magnitude. Whether the loss is material or personal, we are often left with the sense of having been robbed. Rabbi Harold Kushner observed in his bestseller, *When Bad Things Happen to Good People,* that we need to get over the question that focuses on the past and on pain. Instead of asking, "Why did this happen to me?" we need to ask, "Now that this has happened to me, what shall I do about it?" (Stearns 1986, 17).

The encouragement to revitalize latent talents can minimize loss and loneliness. In the Palo Alto senior program, I searched for an older adult piano player who could accompany our sing-a-long sessions. A member informed me about a jazz pianist who had played for a local band. Finally locating Gladys, I discovered a lovely, talented lady who had lost confidence in her ability to perform. I played "Chopsticks" with her on the center's piano, revealing to her that what she had just heard, in one number, was my entire musical repertoire. When I revealed my embarrassment at my inadequacy, her compassionate self emerged, and she began to play the "Twelfth Street Rag" with confidence and enthusiasm.

A few weeks later, after she had located and reviewed her old sheet music, she began to accompany our sing-a-long, led by another senior citizen. Although the song leader could not read music, he could remember all the songs that he had sung in his forties and fifties. Both over age seventy-five adults led the musical program for the three years I lived there and they continued to do so after I moved back East.

As long as we label elderly individuals as unproductive and incompetent, we make their life riskier for vulnerabilities. Instead, if we encourage active and productive living and avoidance of dependency, we strengthen their health (Lehr 1987).

— eight —

DENIAL

"Someday perhaps change will occur when times are ready for it instead of always when it is too late. Someday change will be accepted as life itself."

Shirley MacLaine

Because of the negative attitudes about aging, thoughts and plans for aging are put off as long as possible. The typical attitude is to avoid others who are aging as long as possible, especially the sick, isolated, hospitalized, and those with unpopular roles and status. This attitude makes it more difficult when one finally has to accept aging. It also endorses psychosomatic symptoms and all too often leads directly to low motivation and isolation. Lack of contact with others and total focus on self can lead to escapism or deviance such as promiscuity, alcoholism, other aberrant behavior—even suicide. The suicide rate of older white males, several times that of any other segment of the population, should alert us that it is a time to accept aging changes, reprioritize, and to plan. Refusal to grow old is as foolish as refusal to leave behind one's childhood (Tournier 1972).

Psychological and social denial, individually and collectively, can be documented in almost every phase of the later years of life. Many use denial as a way of coping with anxiety. Denial patterns interfere with the acceptance of aging at all life stages, but especially in old age. Secretiveness about age and overuse of hair dyes, wigs, and cosmetics reflect a personal, culturally determined need to appear young. Physical prowess is exaggerated. Such denials impede healthy adaptation to the reality of aging. A person's defensiveness toward his own aging may well be a dynamic predictor of late-life inability to adapt (Gaitz and Varner 1980).

Research studies document denial as a major instrument in dealing with threats to the self-concept. In a survey of attitudes and behaviors of the elderly, respondents were asked about their experiences as pedestrians during traffic rush hours.

Eighty-five percent stated that they did not have any difficulties crossing streets in dense traffic. On the other hand, 95 percent agreed that all older people are nervous about going onto the streets. Indications were that the respondents did not identify with the lower social status, that of the elderly. Here is denial, not only of one's own age, but also of problems in facing traffic. This reaction was found in almost all men, who, next to children, are the highest risk group of pedestrians in traffic (Thomae 1980).

Another view of denial, however, is when we refuse to see things as they are; instead, we see them as we wish them to be. We tend to think that we can fix an impossible relationship with patience and love; we continue to believe that our efforts can change intolerable behavior in someone if we keep trying and helping. A nosy, bothersome neighbor of mine used to ring the doorbell, hang around on the porch, and was generally a nuisance. I understood that she was lonely without family or close friends in Georgia. I tolerated her behavior until one night she turned into a peeping tom and was staring through my bedroom window when my husband had just returned from a speaking tour. That was the reality that I needed to shake up my relationship with her. I told her to stay off the property, but to call me if she ever had an emergency and needed help.

Dysfunctional relationships in marriage are also difficult to shake, and many women continue to hope that they can change their mate to become a loving father or spouse. Some people do mellow, but many do not. Of course it is difficult to surrender a relationship, but that is not the same as giving up on people.

Death and dying, topics that traditionally have been spoken only in private or have been ignored altogether are, fortunately, no longer taboo. Books, articles, television presentations, and even campus courses have aroused interest in coping with grief, euthanasia, and other subjects related to death. This interest was first acknowledged after the publication of a short story by Leo Tolstoy, "The Death of Ivan Illych." This subject was not freely discussed until Elisabeth Kubler-Ross's book *Death and Dying.* It set in motion a new attitude toward—and awareness of—the needs of people close to death. Self-help groups that recognize the therapeutic value of sharing grief have, in many cases, relieved the fear of talking about death. Ross listened to her dying patients and listed the various stages that a terminally ill person experiences before dying. Similarities were noted in enough people to determine that the following states of mind can be anticipated: denial and isolation, anger, bargaining, depression, and, finally, acceptance (Soudek 1979). Tolstoy's artistic sensibilities allowed him to perceive the same behavior and attitudes associated with death that Ross noted under clinical conditions more than half a century later. Both Tolstoy and Ross tried to view death as a necessary part of life that can be enhanced and made easier if we rid ourselves of fear and anxiety. By examining death, one examines life by understanding, without fear, that life and death are linked to each other. This connection enhances the quality of life. Both Tolstoy and Ross maintained that, to the last breath, we need the loving touch of another human being. Ross's effectiveness as a warm, relating human and pioneer of death therapy may be more significant in the long run than her descriptions of what she saw and heard. Many feel that the reactions of the dying are far more fluid and complex than those she described. The remarkable faculty of terminally ill persons to be able to discuss their death during one period, and then to dismiss the reality completely and speak about being home for a grandchild's graduation or a vacation trip is common. The degrees of denial are never constant (Peterson 1980).

When my own father died, I was driving from Carthage, Tennessee to Knoxville for my very-soon-to-be-son-in-law's graduation from law school, after which we drove on to Wake Forest for my son's graduation. A police car pulled us off the road to tell us that my father had died (I was glad that my family knew where I was going and which route I was taking). Alarmed at the blue light whirling in my rearview mirror, I was shocked at the news. I had spent the night before I left with my father, but could not grasp that he was truly dying. He complained to me, "Sister, I am not doing well." In my uninformed naivete, I just told him he would be fine and went back to sewing Bavarian gifts for my daughter's wedding, as I sat beside his bed. I was preoccupied with details of three graduations and my daughter's imminent wedding. A death was not programmed! I had left a very large Swiss cow bell beside my father's nightstand, after ringing it for him to show him how much noise it made. I had told him that if the nurse didn't come fast enough when he rang the bell, that he should just knock it off the nightstand!

I was sad that the opportunity had slipped away to assure my father that I understood what a wonderful father he had been and that he was responsible for all that I had accomplished. Many times I have thought about the stages of grief that Ross forecast for us, but I simply did not go through these stages. I had been the best daughter I could be under the circumstances and had enjoyed many events with him. I relived those moments in the months that followed.

I would never forget the day he came to me a year earlier and told me that no one had time to take him to the county fair to show his favorite Tennessee walking horse. Not really understanding what I was promising, I agreed that I would help him take his horse to the fair. Little did I realize that I had made a grave mistake. I soon began to understand why no one else had "had the time" to help him. The transport truck for an overactive horse was highly inappropriate—an old wood-rack vintage pickup. We managed to get the horse into the truck and then my father insisted on driving. At age eighty-five, my father's hearing was almost gone and his vision wasn't much better. We managed the one-mile drive to the bridge crossing the Cumberland River off U.S. Highway 70. As we crossed the bridge, the vibrations from the rough concrete and the rickety truck terrified the horse and he tried to climb over the cab of the truck and jump out. I don't believe I have ever felt so close to certain death. Of course, my father could hear almost nothing, and the vibrations we felt he attributed to the roughness of the bridge (which has since been closed for safety reasons)! We did arrive at the Smith County fairgrounds in time for him to saddle the horse and get in the show ring. As the only participant in the class he entered, he came away with a large blue ribbon that he showed to friends near and far until his death, at which time the spirit of his never-say-die optimism had been lifted from his body and passed into my soul.

My dear sister, who had assumed major caregiver responsibility for my father, had brought him home from the hospital at his request. Unfortunately, he declined rapidly and because of the fear that he could die with only her at his side, she called the ambulance to return him to the hospital; he died following readmission. The rapid changes may have contributed to his death in the hospital, where no one wishes to die. Fortunately, my sister remained with him until his last breath.

A form of denial pervades most medical institutions that deal with death, and even families of patients are part of the ritualistic denial system. One wants to believe that a person will not die, or that after they have died, they are not really gone. Beneath the common remarks, "You are looking better today. We are planning a big dinner when you get out," are dogged efforts not to face the fact that the patient is dying. All this may deny the patient the closer relationship with people that sometimes occurs when one is allowed to participate in the acceptance of death. This foreclosure of honesty, of sharing the adventure of death, is the price. In my case, my priorities were unfortunate, but at the time, I simply did not grasp that my never-say-die father could really die. If we could do many things over, it would be different; I would have focused on the life that I was sharing at the moment with him and how very much his love had meant to me. It is not uncommon that the disturbing consequence of our denial of death is the unfinished business that is left behind. Our focus on family and friends and whether or not we have cleared any shadows from the past, such as hurt feelings or words of love unspoken, will leave us with no regrets or guilt feelings.

But how can one be made to believe that a person like my father could die? I had seen him in situations that would kill an ordinary person, but he always recovered. Once just a few years before his death, he had hired prisoners from the local county jail to help him with his farm work, an activity he enjoyed. Connected to the prison system (his business was located across the street from the sheriff's office) and its officials, he requested that an old rusty jail cell be sent to his farm in which to store ears of harvested corn. The rusty cell had been left parked outside the barn and he wanted to use it indoors in the barn, where the corn would be protected from the elements. With his old tractor, he picked up the heavy cell and began to move it. Unbalanced on the tractor's forklift, the cell fell back on his head and damaged his skull. He was diagnosed with a concussion. The doctor alerted his family that he probably would not recover. Wrong! Within a few weeks, he was back in the saddle.

Age and misjudgment were increasingly causing problems, all from which he miraculously recovered. One late night, on the way to the bathroom, he felt his way down the hall from the bedroom. Misjudging an open door to the basement to be the bathroom door, he stepped into the open space and fell twenty steps to the basement. Another concussion sent him to the emergency room; this time, no recovery was predicted for sure. Wrong. In a few months, he was back in the saddle.

He and I were riding horseback through the meadows when he misjudged the fence and ripped open his forearm on barbed wire. Determined to find the cattle that had strayed beyond their fenced area, he stopped, pulled out a piece of twine and a needle (which he had in his saddle bags in case an animal needed quick repair) and sewed up his arm until we could finish what we had set out to do. My cotton scarf served as a temporary tourniquet, and as soon as the cattle had been found, we went to the hospital.

As I sat stunned along the roadside in a steaming hot vehicle in June wondering what to do next, I realized that this man's spirit had finally left his body. In the future, I would always remember how he had overcome handicaps. The descendant of five physician forefathers who had migrated to America to escape the potato famine in Ireland, he was determined that his children would know a better world than he had known. With no education and no financial backing, he had sired and raised nine children, each graduating from college and four with advanced degrees. His love of learning and spirit of entrepreneurship trickled down to his grandchildren who include several physicians, dentists, business gurus, and teachers.

One of my brothers shared his spirit, but has never accepted that aging is a normal part of life or that this stage of life requires caution and care beyond what we earlier practiced. Refusal to repair the floor in his Carthage business led to a fall that caused tremendous damage to his body, and after a short time, a triple bypass. Like my father, he recovered, but it was only after suffering serious health problems that he seemed to realize that he was not what he used to be and had to cautiously move on in life instead of defying caution.

Burial and funeral rites have long provided further evidence of the American's denial of death. The embarrassing expenditures on funerals continue to be purely American. The embalming, cosmetology, and expensive caskets and vaults are calculated to convince survivors that death has been thwarted. The belief that sadness and regrets can be overcome by elaborate farewells is unique to our culture.

However, involvement in the dying process by the family is gradually reemerging. My brother Dave's funeral involved many testimonials of his loving kindness. His early death from lifestyle choices pained all who loved him, but when his good humor and benevolent spirit left his body, many of us felt deeper commitment to encourage those who misunderstand the need for good habits that preserve instead of destroy.

A special, caring approach to dying, the hospice movement, originally directed at the terminally ill, enables older people to die at home. The aim of this movement is to remove distressful symptoms of dying in the expectation that what remains of a person's life can be used and enjoyed. My brother Ray, who was undoubtedly the recipient of my mother's benevolent spirit, was the kindest human I had ever known. When I saw him being spoon-fed at a u-shaped table in a nursing home, I was offended and infuriated that such a wonderful human could be left to share probably the only enjoyable aspect of life—food—in such an unloving way. My other brother Frank had remained at home when diagnosed with Alzheimer's. His dedicated wife, whose life revolved totally around him, slept when he did, ate when he did, and stayed by his side day and night. Although she never complained, he did not suffer in the last years of his life like most victims of Alzheimer's disease. When her children noticed

146

that the caregiving burden was contributing to her decline, the four adult male children took turns sleeping beside him on alternative nights, allowing their mother to rest. I always believed that their loving care prevented him from becoming violent or incontinent because he lived a decent, pleasant family life at home until the end.

An attack on lavish and costly burials happens more frequently now, and it has also made death and dying a less forbidden subject. It is becoming common to take control by choosing memorial services made more personal by featuring readings by family and close friends, by making living wills, by participating in thanology courses (courses about the fear of death and dying), self-help groups, and the hospice movement—and to choose lower-cost alternatives to funerals. The total number of cremations has doubled, reflecting the public's growing desire to hold down costs. Making choices prior to death's emotional turmoil is reflected in the number of prepaid funerals. While the trend away from showy funerals is applauded, many fear that the swift disposal of a body from the place of death to the crematory—a practice that occurs in 20 percent of all deaths in some parts of the West—denies the reality of death and ignores the fact that a life has been led (Maloney 1983). When I was called to eulogize the death of one of my senior friends in Palo Alto, I remember the uneasiness I felt when I approached the table where her little box of ashes had been placed. That was all that was left of Flora, who had been dancing with us at Senior Friendship Days just a week earlier. It was a very disturbing revelation about the fragility of life and the urge to make every moment of human encounter a piece of eternity. The opportunity to see, to speak to, to smile, or to share with another person again is never guaranteed. Flora had vanished; only memories of her altruism and energy at Senior Friendship Days remained. Her spirit is what we remembered.

We continue to deny, because denial is but one way to preserve some degree of mental sanity in the face of our demise. Anger, and even rage, may be more comforting, and perhaps more productive, than denial. If one can handle the emotional turmoil through engagement in self improvement, that could be a step in the right direction to developing a more mature mental adjustment to death. Kubler-Ross (1969) fails, however, to define either the value of rage or its justification. Catharsis through the expression of anger may disturb those around us, but it can be an integrating experience. Repressed anger, as one contemplates loss of self and loss of loved ones, can be destructive when it surfaces later. It may be justification at the time for coming closer to dealing with the reality of death.

As early as 1872, Darwin described grief as essentially a biological process that, at times, jeopardizes the life of the organism. Research, combined with Darwin's observations, has postulated a biological theory of grief, stressing the physical impact of loss on people's lives. Loss can disrupt the emotional, intellectual, spiritual, and physical aspects of people's lives (Schneider 1984).

Highly consistent actuarial data has shown that the loss of a prior human relationship is related to virtually every major disease from cancer to mental illness, with a particularly strong link to heart disease. The people most prone to premature death from heart disease are the widowed, divorced, separated, old and single, young and living alone, and children from broken homes. Loss can be a factor in major and developmental illnesses as well as being significant to minor illnesses, including colds and flu. Anxiety, depression, and insomnia, as well as arthritis and rheumatoid conditions, are prominent symptoms following loss (Schneider 1984).

Some experts believe that terrible disturbances of the life pattern, such as divorce, death of the spouse or of a close friend, or loss of a job, do not occur often enough to be the cause of many chronic illnesses. The accumulation of little daily hassles are more often seen as the cause of illnesses. A hassles scale, with items ranging from major problems, such as retirement—to minor annoyances such as inconsiderate smokers, losing things, concern over money, or being lonely— lists what really may be a greater cause of illness. The major events most often seen as causing illnesses may be of less importance in terms of causing disease than the occurrence of chronic daily hassles. A ten-month study on hassles and uplift (the importance of adaptation to daily events as compared to life crises) indicated that the overwhelming disturbance caused by little ongoing daily hassles can be more damaging than major catastrophic events (Whitbourne 1985).

Forcing our own hopeful spirits onto those who are grieving and have begun to reject their own self-worth can be discouraging. If we deny their real pain and despair, we may run the risk of destroying even the tiny amount of light that is left in their lives. One of my technicians, Donnie, rushed to my office immediately after the death of his mother. Grieving over her death, he was stricken with lack of direction of how to handle his grief. He suddenly remembered that my brother had died just a couple of days previously, and he began to apologize for bothering me with his grief. I convinced him that suffering was acceptable, and that my grief should not interfere with the sorrow he felt for his mother. I assured him that my suffering should not detract him from his own, that it was okay for him to grieve, and that our sharing had lightened the burden for both of us.

Extensive evidence documents the negative consequences when loss is ignored. Subsequent losses are less likely to be resolved, and energy remains a captive to the loss. If unresolved losses are allowed to accumulate, gradual disheartening and emotional poverty can result. Losses must be faced, thought about, and confronted (Tombs 1984).

Each of us has the right and responsibility to take our losses seriously. Grief, when ignored or denied, can harm us in countless ways. When we face our losses, we can find our freedom again. We must give ourselves time to grieve. Just how long it takes depends on the circumstances of the loss. Many grieve the slow death or gradual deterioration of a marriage for a long time, and only a few weeks of emotional turmoil may follow divorce. However, when death comes suddenly, or when people are forced to deal with radical surgery, a debilitating accident, or other unforeseen tragedy, the mourning can last a year or longer. Successful adaptation to grief can increase one's ability to experience life fully. The final phase of the grief process can transform loss into a growth experience. Grief can be transmuted into creative energy (Stearns 1986).

— nine —

COPING—THE KEY TO ADJUSTMENT IN LATER LIFE

"Emotion, which is suffering, ceases to be suffering as soon as we form a clear and precise picture of it."

Benedict de Spinoza in *The Ethics*

Coping gradually becomes a central theme in old age. It is an ongoing transaction between situational demands and actively perceiving, appraising, and acting on them. In addition to having to cope with the necessity of remaining active and retaining functions, the older adult must deal with identity review of self. Some older persons continue to use the entire range of adaptive mechanisms; some may regress to the use of defense mechanisms. Failure to adapt to challenging or threatening demands occurs more frequently. Depression, withdrawal, extreme anxiety, blaming others, denial, and focusing on aches and pains—real or imagined—may interfere with coping capacities.

Regardless of one's age, effort is needed to manage the demands of daily living. Restoring order to life following a stressful event, with the goal of reestablishing the status quo, may be compounded by other losses. Because our environment and capabilities change as we age, so do our coping capacities. Good coping allows us to link primary motivations with ultimate resolutions of problems getting in our way.

In the Bonn Longitudinal Study on Aging (BLSA), patterns of coping with occupational problems over two decades showed a meaningful cognitive and behavioral restructuring in aging participants. For example, identification with the successes and goals of children and grandchildren became stronger as coping strategies changed. A study of changing social role activities and satisfaction showed little or no decrease in scores measuring activity and satisfaction, unless there were health conditions that interfered. A reordering of priorities and a change in the thematic structure of role behavior seems to occur. While institutionalized activities decrease in relevance, the informal ones that fulfill the aging individual's needs seem to remain important (Olbrich 1986).

Comparisons of styles of coping with health problems encountered over the timespan of the BLSA suggested that aging persons structure their situations in a way that allows them to deal meaningfully with loss and failure. Data from medical examinations showed that health problems increase as people age, especially the symptoms of heart insufficiency and sclerosis, as well as high blood pressure. The overall intensity of coping with housing problems, economic troubles, and family conflicts showed a remarkable consistency over a ten-year period. There is evidence that, over a lifetime, there was a reordering of priorities, a relegation of no-longer-relevant roles to the periphery of importance, and an investment in activities more in tune with present commitments as well as changes in coping styles. Achievement techniques did not decrease, but relying on others became more important. Old parents continued to support the households of their children finan-cially and to give care, while taking support as needed from their social environment (Olbrich 1986).

In some healthy persons, judgment, wisdom, and the ability to think through and solve problems does not always deteriorate;

many mature adults become more altruistic and are capable of sublimating some earlier drives. It has been my experience that an increase in advanced common sense is often seen in older adults, but wisdom is not necessarily related to chronological age. Many younger people seem to mature earlier than some of their elders. However, older adults seem to be more capable of resolving practical problems than younger adults.

There are various explanations for why aging individuals prefer and develop different ways of coping and different lifestyles. Some psychologists believe that genetics predispose people to be naturally active participants in life, while others are just as naturally engaged in passive observation. The phrase "flight or fight" describes characteristic styles of coping among some older people. Some elders simply turn away from the demands of life and take flight. Others typically face life by fighting back. Some take action at times and withdraw at others. Weisman emphasizes the importance of maintaining hope under all circumstances. He writes, "Hope must prevail. Hope means that special values, unique to the aged, are there to be pursued and fulfilled" (1986, 146).

Stress resulting from the need to secure benefits in retirement may call up defenses. When I was in a difficult higher education work environment, the threat of retiring early was always present.

A very close friend, Beulah, whose sister had experienced many medical expenses in retirement, chided me for even considering early retirement. She told me about the health benefits of her sister in retirement from the Georgia University system where I taught. She advised me to write the word retirement on my chest and look at it every day for another year, when I would qualify for retirement benefits. I remembered her advice, when at a local university, a staff employee came to my office and threw the overdue paperwork in my garbage can and yelled, "Noncompliance!" When two laptop computers were stolen from my desk, departure from my office was appealing. The stress of an unknown future of healthcare inspired me again to imagine the word "retirement" written on my chest. I learned to cope by swimming more than my usual twenty laps in the pool those evenings, finally being tired enough to sleep soundly and prepare for another day to put out fires at the office.

From a historical point of view, there have been several broad perspectives for current approaches to coping with life crises. Charles Darwin's evolutionary theory emphasized the relationship of the ability to cope to the environment. Darwin taught that humans are interdependent and must make collective efforts to survive. This orientation leads to an emphasis on behavioral problem-solving activities and coping strategies that enhance not only the survival of the individual, but also the species (Moos and Schaefer 1986).

Sigmund Freud's theories led us to believe that behavior results from the drive to satisfy sexual and aggressive instincts. Our subconscious ego processes help reduce tension between individual impulses and the constraints of external reality. Later, psychologists rejected Freud's ideas, declaring that healthy individuals are capable of controlling their behavior, their lives, and their environments.

At one time, it was thought that life events in infancy determined adult personality. Later information about the growth of ego functions and normal patterns of maturation showed that early life events do not necessarily foreshadow a person's character or pattern of reactions to crises and transitions (Moos and Schaefer 1986). The gradual acquisition of resources over a lifetime and an understanding of the stages of development are the most frequently encountered explanations of how we manage the life course. Erikson describes the eight stages of human development, their tasks, and the inner quality experienced in each stage. Each stage encompasses a crisis that must be successfully negotiated to adequately cope with the next stage. Coping resources are thus built to resolve subsequent crises. Personal coping styles developed early in life are, however, apt to be carried over into old age. Reaching old age without having to confront major life crises, or failing to resolve such crises, may be responsible for inadequate coping mechanisms in later life (Erikson, Erikson, and Kivnik 1986).

In-depth studies of adaptation under extreme conditions of misery, pain, and discontent have sparked renewed insight into human competence and coping. Inmates in concentration camps have experienced the most hellish degradation ever endured by mankind. Few of our fellow men opted for suicide under such conditions. Even there, many inmates managed to salvage some control. Viktor Frankl's experiences in Nazi prison camps showed how some persons were resistant to daily inhumane treatment. A 2008 report on survival under extreme stress suggests that "locus of control" may explain why some people appear to be able to cope well through good and bad circumstances. Those with an external focus think that outside forces (forces outside the person being affected) or random happenings are the reason they can't cope. Findings suggest that those with a strong internal locus of control are more likely to cope with everyday activities. For example, Gonzales (2008) contrasts the results of a study of Alabama residents with Illinois residents. Alabama residents believed their fate was controlled by God, not by them. The study indicated that the

Illinois respondents were more inclined to have confidence in their own abilities, and to take action. He suggests that we should balance confidence with reasonable doubt and self-esteem with self-criticism every single day. The stress of coping with everyday hassles can be attenuated as we develop self-confidence and an "internal locus of control" (Gonzales 2008).

Individuals who have faced and resolved severe problems may find that they have increased self-esteem, are able to perform better in similar situations at a later time, learn empathy, and can take advantage of new opportunities. In fact, life transitions and crises can provide essential conditions for psychological development. Stressful episodes can enrich a person's beliefs and values by making it necessary to assimilate new experiences. Overcoming demanding and difficult changes contributes to a continuing development in old age. Many persons experiencing life crises remain healthy and thus develop resistance resources that may help to prevent stress or to manage it effectively (Weisman 1984).

Keeping one's emotional balance in the face of a crisis is advantageous. When stress overwhelms us, we have trouble remembering and carrying out tasks. It should not be embarrassing to forget someone's name or to be unable to recall where we placed an item that we need. Remaining calm and reflecting on some feature of the person or on what preceded the lapse of memory will provide a better chance of recall. When we are anxious, we are simply more likely to fail.

Whether stressful demands will lead to growth, temporary difficulty, or trauma in the individual is determined by the pervasiveness and persistence of the stressor; the timing of the event; the individual's personal resources available for dealing with the stressor; the opportunities available to act on the environment and to receive social support; and the meaning given to the experience (Olbrich 1986).

The way in which the individual appraises his or her relationship to the environment and its stressful factors determines the emotional reaction. Cognitive therapy teaches patients to identify challenges and to adopt alternative ways to view themselves and their situations. How people use their minds to solve problems—or to create or aggravate them—determines to a large extent whether one will fully recover, just survive, or will enjoy life (Birren and Renner 1980).

Following a complicated rotator cuff surgery, coping with the subsequent pain of physical therapy was possible only through self-prescribed cognitive therapy. As I tried to recover the use of my right arm, I would psyche myself up by using my brain to distract me from the numerous painful exercises necessary to restore movement. With the ultimate goal of being able to hook my own bra again, during therapy I would count to one hundred in German, then try to remember how to do the same in Spanish. This latter mental challenge proved very difficult; I had not used my Spanish skills for three or more decades. I would also relive pleasant experiences, pretending that I was scuba diving, dancing with my best partner, or trying to chronologically log travels that I had experienced throughout my life. This technique proved so successful that my benevolent physical therapist said she was going to go back to school and take hypnosis so she could help other patients do what I had successfully managed. Recovery was total and hooking my bra was achieved!

Cooperation with the physician, the therapist, the teacher, or with whomever the challenger is, is necessary to accomplish improvement. Joint efforts are more likely to be successful to change behavior. Improvement of functional capabilities and expansion of social capital (friends, relationships with others) frequently enhances coping abilities.

The inevitability of our demise may pose the greatest challenge. Survivors who are able to find meaning in their bereavement may experience growth rather than despair. In other words, facing a fate he cannot change, a person may rise above himself, may grow beyond himself, and in so doing, may change himself. He may turn a personal tragedy into a triumph. Frankl relates how he forced his thoughts to turn to another world when he became disgusted with the state of affairs in the prison camp that compelled him to think only of trivial things and survival. In this way he succeeded in rising above the situation, above the sufferings and deaths of the moment, and observed them as if they were already of the past. His troubles became the object of an interesting psycho-scientific study undertaken by himself (Kimble and Ellor 1989).

Spiritual needs are identified as the "deepest requirements of the self" which, when met, make it possible for the person to function with a meaningful identity and purpose—so that in all stages of life, that person may relate to reality with hope. These needs include the need for identity, meaning, love, and wisdom. Spiritual needs may be met by a religious act, such as praying or receiving Holy Communion, but many spiritual needs are met by warm and sympathetic human relationships. Failure to recognize that man is a spiritual being and failure to meet social needs leads to indignities and injustices (Agostino 1988).

My next door neighbor, Evelyn, age eighty-four, has a posse of friends who provide transportation to church and social activities when she cannot or does not wish to drive. Recently,

I delivered dinner to her when she was very ill. The next morning when I looked out my window, it was 20 degrees, and her car windows were covered with ice. She scraped off the windows and headed for church. Determined to stay independent, her church and community activities seem to bring joy and meaning to her life. Like many older folks, she regards religion as very important, especially during special religious holidays. She is a music lover and around holidays she is preoccupied with her church choir and church activities. The preparation for these significant religious holidays and her ongoing connections to her choir members seem to boost her immune system.

Another friend, Nell, is not associated with any particular religion, but at age eighty-nine is just as active and healthy as my neighbor. Nell is only found inside a church when there is a family wedding, christening, or funeral. I consider her very spiritual, without a special focus on church. She portrays the horizontal dimension of spirituality, which extends throughout ordinary life experiences and through lifelong learning. Aware of every opportunity to improve herself, she engages any spare time in continuing education courses. She is politically engaged, as well as being the neighbor who collects funds for cancer, arthritis, and any charity that calls on her. She copes with caring for her physician husband, a victim of dementia, by staying involved in limited external activities.

Yet another person whose religious beliefs help her with daily struggles is my sister Mary. Mary is an angel to everyone, and she expects to join the archangels and her family when she passes away (her description of her death). She knows where she is headed, and St. Peter will be fortunate to have her join his angels. She claims that she has already seen heaven and the anticipation of that destination appears to make her difficult present life bearable. She clearly represents the vertical dimension of religion that reaches toward God (McFadden 2005). Not that she is killing time—she cares for her husband, her frail sister, and her church members, and she prepares meals for unexpected visitors from near and far communities where her husband formerly pastored Baptist churches. She has had more than one near-death experience that gives meaning and promise to her life. When I ask her about her near-death experiences, she radiates joy and satisfaction. No, she is not hallucinating. Physician Melvin Morse endorses her beliefs and states that scientific research reveals an area of the brain where these experiences really happen, and that these experiences are normal and natural, not caused by psychological processes or lack of oxygen to the brain. He describes astonishment at how love and thoughts of love are experienced by everyone who returns from near death experiences. "Those who have returned from seeing God bring a simple message—we create our surroundings by the thoughts that we think. We are sent here to live life fully, to find joy in our creations, to experience and magnify our lives . . . to love, to be kind, to be tolerant, to give generous service" (Eadie 1992, 2).

German has two different words for what we Americans think when we speak of spirituality: *Geistig* refers to our ability to transcend ourselves, our spirituality; *geistlich* refers to our relationship with God (Teague et al. 1997). Unfortunately, we have a preconceived notion of what spirituality is all about. I have known very spiritual people who were not identified with any religion and very religious persons who were not spiritual. Mary is my example of *geistlich,* or identification with God; Nell is an example of *geistig,* a spiritual person, although not identified with a religion. My neighbor, Evelyn, personifies both religion and spirituality. Although both religion and spirituality emphasize love, joy, peace, sense of purpose, and achieving one's full potential, there are limitations in how these are built into our lives. While both views are important to health and a well-managed lifestyle, the problem is that the word "spiritual" may create fear of indoctrination into a religious experience. Another problem is the belief that spiritual health is an end in itself, instead of a process of becoming. Spirituality is the need within to develop to the best of our ability. That said, relationships and bonds with other people are priorities because we cannot know a higher level of life without being involved in the lives of others, especially in helping others achieve fulfillment. It is positive and healthy to have a perfect model to relate to, as we do in supreme beings. Hopefully, we will remember that example when faced with ethical and moral decisions. Whether these decisions revolve around relationships, health, or use of time and resources, they are more likely to add value to our lives when we ask ourselves, "How would my God resolve this problem or make this decision?" Or, some may ask, "How would my ideal person, be it a family member, or another role model, solve this dilemma?" When we are searching for answers and truth, prayer and meditation can be helpful to some; others, like the Illinois folks in the research mentioned previously, are more likely to have confidence in their own abilities, and to take action.

The energy that we need to seek answers to ultimate questions may come from spirituality or from religion. Spirituality is an integration of body, mind, and spirit and transcends our personal thoughts of self. I find this is very important because of the need to see things as they really are and to face the trials and tribulations of late life with an open mind and heart.

Freedom results from a total acceptance of our aging and that freedom opens our heart to more love and acceptance of others unlike ourselves. We grow best when we face challenges, overcome them, and learn to live with them.

Author Scott Peck states that there is no distinction between the process of achieving spiritual growth and achieving mental growth. He states that the problem underlying continuous personal growth is simply laziness (1978). The spiritual persons I have known appear to have unlimited energy for personal growth, and for the search for truth.

Religion, on the other hand, comforts more than challenges. Religion is more of a social institution organized around a doctrine in which we are trained throughout life. There are thousands of religious groups, each promoting that their beliefs are the only acceptable ones. Narrow and intolerant religious beliefs have led to conflict and have destroyed as many people as they have helped. Although it comforts many people, religion also causes many to suffer. It often encourages a closed mind without examining beliefs of millions of other persons. Religion continues, however, to be helpful to many who are coping with a crisis. Carl Jung considered "religiosity" in man not a symptom of a neurosis, but a possible cure. According to Jung, man is driven by his religious instincts, but according to Frankl, man reaches out by his own decision. Other existential psychologists see religion as the proper concern of the healthy man.

Abraham Maslow considers one sick who is unconcerned with religion. Personal awareness of the superhuman dimension can give the individual assurance that order exists, and that he personally has a place in that order. One can see order in the world in humanistic terms or in terms of ultimate meaning. Science, too, rests on the assumption that the universe hangs together. Religion and spirituality aid in developing the coping skills that can lead to satisfaction in late life (Fabry 1968).

Coping with hunger in the Nazi prison camps exposed a diversity of coping skills, unmasking both the beast and the saint. Dr. Frankl reported that, unlike the expectation that individual differences would blur when prisoners were starving, people became more diverse. The hunger was the same for everyone, but different coping reactions were unmasked. The sensitive people who were accustomed to a rich intellectual life may have suffered much pain in concentration camps because of their delicate constitution, but the damage to their inner selves was less. Some prisoners of a less hardy makeup seemed to survive the prison camp life better than those of a robust nature; they were able to retreat from their terrible surroundings to a life of inner riches and spiritual freedom. The intensification of inner life helped prisoners find a refuge from the emptiness, desolation, and spiritual poverty of existence by providing an escape into the past or planning for their future (Frankl 1984).

The coping ability of an individual under stress is increasingly understood as a function of personal resources, as measured against deficits, at the time the event occurs. Resources, including health, psychological and social traits, age, gender, and socioeconomic status appear to be moderators of reaction to life's events in adulthood. A person's beliefs and patterns of commitment, as well as social restraints, also affect how that person responds to stress and is able to cope. The simultaneous occurrence of several negative events tends to have long-term effects on individuals lacking resources. An extensive array of strategies, rather than just a few that are not flexible, are used by good copers. Financial security is more important for men, and social participation is more critical for women as a measurement of coping (Whitbourne 1985, 172).

Author Robert Butler has drawn attention to reminiscing about previous life events as a means of coping. However, reminiscing may have positive or negative effects. The reorganization of life's experiences can lead to a more insightful understanding of a person or may result in depression with reality-based or imagined guilt feelings. Some aged individuals become more serene through the use of life review. Being able to see in writing what one's life has been may be convincing that it is enough. Some realize that to be accepted, more is not always necessary (Moos and Schaefer 1986).

However, recollection may not be as rewarding as are efforts to form new relationships. Focusing on the future, on fulfillment of the individual in the future, and on responsibility for the time remaining can encourage accomplishment and happiness. Persons who cope best with the diminishments of growing older are those who have a meaningful plan for the future. In the prisoner-of-war camps (in Japan, North Korea, and North Vietnam, as well as in the Nazi concentration camps), one could witness that those who knew that there was a task waiting for them to fulfill in the future were most apt to survive. Yale University School of Medicine researchers observed a number of Vietnam War prisoners who explicitly claimed that they had benefited from the captivity experience, seeing it as a growth experience.

The Danish existentialist Søren Kierkegaard emphasized openness to the future as central to the confirmation of life's goals in the second half of life. Trust in our revitalization capacity opens up expectations. Kierkegaard stressed that it is important to remain aware that one has already accomplished something, without losing one's openness and ability to grow and develop in the future. Anticipation based on creative thoughts must never be given up. Action is the opportunity of life.

Many famous people lived long lives working on masterpieces. Johann Wolfgang von Goethe worked seven years completing the second part of *Faust*. Finally, in January 1832, he sealed the manuscript; two months later he died. His orientation toward the future may have had lifesaving effects, delaying death until shortly after completion of Faust. Goethe showed his wisdom with the words: "We must always aim at the bull's eye, although we will not always hit it. We have to try to reach the absolutely best—otherwise we shall not even reach the relatively good" (Frankl 1967, 17). My own father used to ask me why my report card didn't have a note of 100 instead of a note of 95 or higher. What had I not done to get less than a perfect score was his smiling admonition!

Mark Twain used humor as a relief mechanism to cope. His most significant works came after the death of his infant child. He later stated, "The human race has but one effective weapon, and that is laughter." Appropriate humor can help with life-threatening illness. If people can laugh at themselves, at how seriously they take themselves, then they can begin to gain perspective, to heal, and to reformulate total tragedy into new forms of energy. Immanuel Kant, in his *Critique of Pure Reason* wrote that laughter produced "a feeling of health through the furtherance of the vital bodily processes." Likewise, Freud believed that mirth was a highly useful mechanism to counteract nervous tension, and that humor could be used as an effective therapy. Sir William Osler regarded laughter as the "music of life." William Fry of Stanford University wrote a highly illuminating paper, "The Respiratory Components of Mirthful Laughter." Like Kant, he found that the entire process of respiration is benevolently engaged by laughter. Author and unflagging optimist Norman Cousins used humor to show that the human mind can order the body to react or respond in certain ways (Cousins 1979).

Humor can stimulate the release of endorphins. Individuals with determination to overcome an illness tend to have a greater tolerance of severe pain than those who are morbidly apprehensive. Chinese scientists maintain that acupuncture activates the endorphins and can be used as an anesthetic. A Japanese doctor who incorporated laughter into the treatment of tuberculosis patients was able to demonstrate to his own satisfaction that laughter was therapeutic.

Norman Doidge in his 2007 book, *The Brain that Changes Itself,* documents this powerful use of the mind in the story of

Bach y Rita. Rita suffered a massive stroke which disabled him physically and mentally. With the help of his dedicated medical student son, he fully recovered use of all faculties. At autopsy, the areas of his brain damaged by the stroke were obvious, but other areas of the brain had assumed the tasks of some sections that were seriously damaged or destroyed. Rita's motivation to heal had set in motion changes in the brain that remapped areas that took over tasks of other areas of the brain that had been damaged.

Helping others provides a sense of purpose and is a way for the bereaved and victimized to find meaning in their suffering. Reaching out to others, being extroverted, adding acquaintances at every opportunity—all are beneficial to aging. Carl Menninger advised that when a person felt a nervous breakdown coming on, he or she should find someone in need and do something to help that person. In addition to volunteering, self-help groups may also be vehicles for emotional and problem-focused coping on an individual or community level (Moos and Schaefer 1986).

Once, after Frankl lectured at Melbourne University, he was given an Australian boomerang for a souvenir. As he was told, a boomerang comes back to the hunter only when it has missed its target. He believed that, ideally, man also should return to himself and be concerned with himself only after he has missed his mission and has failed to find a meaning in his life.

One strategy for coping with the monumental changes of aging is to renew assault on one's goals—a new burst of devotion focused on achievement, whether in the halls of science, the market place, or the more private world of sex.

Psychologist Florida Scott-Maxwell said at a very advanced age: "Our whole duty may be to clarify and increase what we are, to make our consciousness a finer quality. The efforts of one's entire life are needed if we are to return laden to our source" (1968, 40).

Expectations may seem demanding of the elderly in contrast to the fun and games image of the later years that businesses and institutions have tried to sell. Continued contributions to society could help resolve many of society's problems, including the apathy of many older adults, whose passive use of precious time increases the risk of depression and disease. Educational activities can develop inner resources, help a person develop a sense of integrity in his or her life, and thus enable the person to transcend the stresses associated with old age. Participation in the arts and art education can provide older persons with avenues for self-expression that open up new vistas of achievement, new roles, and new interests. All this serves to compensate for some of the social, physical, and emotional losses many older people experience. Continuing education, whether in the arts, music, languages, or technology, is a valuable way to transcend the stresses of old age. It is possible that the anxiety associated with the realization of the limitation of time, and with the frenetic need to crowd old or new conquests into the few remaining years, may be factors in the startling heart attack rates experienced in the industrialized Western world.

Stressful episodes may enrich a person's beliefs and values by making it necessary to assimilate new experiences. Life crises can initiate the development of new cognitive and personal skills, primarily because such skills are needed for successful adaptation in late life. Florida Scott-Maxwell states that the hardiness of life she deplores creates the qualities she admires. The efficient mastering of demanding and different situations contributes to a broadening of behavioral potentialities and a continuing development in old age. We must cope "well enough and nurture morale high enough to endure disappointment and despair" (Scott-Maxwell 1968, 41).

Taking advantage of opportunities may lower the negative effects of stress. The Chinese use the character that identifies crisis to make this point. The character consists of two parts: the first part, standing alone, means danger; the second, standing alone, indicates opportunity. The two characters together mean crisis. This could be interpreted to mean that there may be more opportunities (since there are more strokes in the second character) in a crisis than there are dangers (Lesnoff-Caravaglia 1985).

Hillary Clinton's resolution of the infidelity of the former president is a prime example. Many women would not have chosen to remain married to Bill, but Hillary clearly saw the opportunities in the crisis, and she minimized the dangers to her family. When many spouses might not have been capable of forgiving and moving on, she showed strength, understanding, and courage in their marital crisis, moving forward to become a senator and then secretary of state. Had she focused on danger instead of opportunity, she surely would have had a comfortable financial settlement, but she might never have been elevated to her present status, nor perhaps would her daughter have remained emotionally strong. She renegotiated a contract with her partner, which at the end of the day may have been easier than initiating a new contract with someone else.

There are many examples of unparalleled strength in overcoming crisis. The biblical story of Samson's slaying of the lion whose carcass later served as a repository for bees exemplifies this idea. The bees made the desert-dehydrated carcass a home and used it for depositing honey. Samson later used the honey to his advantage. Creating honey from a lion is what many older women do. The power struggle of many older men can ruin a marriage and weaken ties to children and grandchildren. The acceptance of waning strength and interdependence with others and with the environment can provide an atmosphere of growth that diminishes the need to overpower others.

A person who has led a fulfilled life and has overcome challenges will be much better prepared to master the problems and crises that lie ahead. Sigmund Freud expressed this in a single sentence: "*Wenn du leben willst, bereite dich aud den tod*" (If you really want to live, prepare yourself for death).

— ten —

SUCCESSFUL AGING IN RETIREMENT—RETIREMENT PRECEDES AGING; AGING PRECEDES DEATH

"Will you still need me, will you still feed me,

when I'm sixty-four?"

Paul McCartney

Each of us wants to age successfully. When asked what successful aging is, a common response is "free of pain." However, many older adults who are aging successfully have just as many aches and pains as friends who are not aging so well. The difference in whether or not we will be able to cope with inevitable changes depends, in large part, on our coping skills and resilience.

Retirement often brings into question values for which one is not prepared. The question may arise: "If you are what you do, what are you when you don't do what you did?" After retirement, a person who has identified mainly with work may experience unanticipated changes. The more or less involuntary departure from work forces many to seek a meaningful life. Finding a retirement interpretation of self can be very difficult. The loss of roles precipitates identity crises, especially for men whose identity depended entirely on their career. This role loss often leads to a central lack of meaning in retirement.

In anticipation of retirement and subsequent aging, what knowledge, insight, behavior, and talents should one learn and develop to lead a full and enriched later life? First of all, aging successfully means taking on the responsibility for one's own lifestyle. Changes in the various organs and tissues can lead to loss of strength, but can be influenced through preventive health measures. The realization that we are more vulnerable to physical decline as we age should motivate us to necessary changes.

Change is fundamental to life in retirement, and change will accelerate as we age. Alterations to the environment, body, and brain should be anticipated. Change can be very stressful, and if we learn to let go and to adjust to changes, quality of life will be more enjoyable. The very first change that perplexes us is what a friend of mine calls "Ter-ror-nesia" (terror-knees-ia), a word she created to describe a form of terror she has experienced. She describes this as the panic that occurs when you begin to introduce two people you know to each other and you suddenly forgot both of their names and your knees buckle!

Minor memory lapses are, indeed, bothersome, and all of us have experienced them. The good news is that some memory changes are normal, and it is important that we are not overly concerned when minor lapses occur—such as when we go to the telephone and forget whom we were planning to call! Memory loss does not result primarily from aging. Depression, low blood sugar, anemia and lung disease, small strokes, poor blood circulation, head injuries, fluid imbalance, drug overdoses, interactions of prescription drugs with over-the-counter drugs or with herbal medicines, malnutrition and other health-related and social conditions—all can affect brain function.

When hard pressed to remember something, we should relax. Instead of becoming nervous and apologizing that we forgot, it is perfectly acceptable to say, "I cannot think of it now," "It did not register," or, "I was not paying attention."

When we relax and quit worrying, we can usually recall what we wished to remember. We are more likely to remember when we trust and accept ourselves and don't get embarrassed.

Keeping the mind challenged through book clubs, adult education courses, and the pursuit of knowledge or new experiences are ways to retain memory. Relearning any subject that we had previously mastered can be exhilarating. Recalling information that has not been used for decades is stimulating. When we relearn something it is "greasing the pathways" previously laid down in our brains. A pathway in the brain that we have already established makes subsequent learning easier. That's why we should keep reviewing or relearning anything that we have previously learned, even though it may have been learned decades before. In retirement, we can find the time to do just that. Natural memory loss can be regained, but it takes effort. Sensory awareness is critical; it is our senses that transfer information to the brain. Keeping glasses clean and hearing aids cleaned and repaired, keeping the hearing channels free of wax—these simple tasks are critical, since the eyes and ears provide input to the brain.

Visual reminders in one's environment are helpful. When we park our cars, it may be necessary to record the street or place where we parked. Paying bills the same day they arrive, or completing tasks the same day they are started, lowers the chances of neglecting them. Practicing simple tricks to help us remember can be very helpful. Mnemonics (the Greek work for memory aids) have been used for decades. For example, "Spring forward, fall back," when we adjust our clocks to and from daylight saving time. Such organization and practice of what we wish to remember helps encode the information in the brain, making it easier to recall ("Thirty days hath September . . . "). The bottom line is to keep your mind active, your body healthy, and your spirit alive through community and family involvement. And, don't let yourself be a victim of terror-nesia—don't panic when you can't remember something. As long as minor lapses of memory do not interfere with basic functioning, we have little reason for concern.

It is important for everyone to work out every kind of problem in each phase of life and not carry them as unresolved ballast into the next phase of life. It is not true that they lose their relevance later on, that one can hide them, or that one can work out the feelings of guilt that will inevitably appear. In good times, these difficult problems superficially remain, but in time of instability, weakened physical strength and diminished self-confidence, unresolved problems often unintentionally surface. As the Germans say: *Man muss das Eisen schmieden, solange es heiss ist* (One must forge the iron while it is still hot). One should not put off dealing with problems. This is a basic tenet of preventive geriatric psychiatry.

Above all, it is difficult at the beginning of retirement to find meaningful, motivating goals and new ways of life. One notices this especially in today's churches, where customs and traditions are not as strong. Historically, a person could take part in all phases of life in the church and within family circles. This participation made it much easier to find meaning in life. Now, the rapid progress of science and technology leaves many older adults feeling old fashioned, and can lead to withdrawal and to distrust of new developments. Some scientists believe that the technical progress that has lengthened life does not provide the quality of life that an older person anticipates. The diagram below indicates the many changes to the individual lifespan that a person experiences in the twentieth century. Adjusting to the technological and cultural

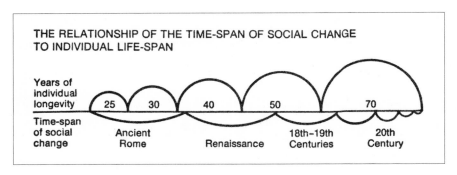

THE RELATIONSHIP OF THE TIME-SPAN OF SOCIAL CHANGE TO INDIVIDUAL LIFE-SPAN

Years of individual longevity — 25   30   40   50   70

Time-span of social change — Ancient Rome   Renaissance   18th–19th Centuries   20th Century

changes in the past century has challenged many older adults beyond their ability to adjust (Knowles 1974, 41).

An ongoing mastery of new technology is necessary for young and old to thwart loss of connections among friends, family, and the outside world. Constant training and lifelong continuing education are doubtless necessary and build on acquired knowledge and experience. Obsolete thinking and lack of knowledge ages us faster than is necessary. Rapid progress in technology outpaces the existing knowledge of all age groups, and requires more energy by older adults to stay alert and informed. The relationship of the time-span of social change to individual lifespan is clearly shown in Dr. Malcolm Knowles's diagram on the previous page. It is very difficult for many seniors to adjust to such rapid changes in technology, along with all the other energy-draining adjustments of aging. Although it is surprising how rapidly some seniors adjust and wish to learn new technical skills, we cannot blame those who do not wish to or cannot.

New relationships, new challenges, and new lifestyles can add to our quality of life and can expand our minds. When George Bernard Shaw stated that an "eternal vacation is a living hell," he was implying that living in eternal comfort zones can be damaging. Comfort zones can dull our brains. Recently, a couple of architect designers created homes that challenged the persons who purchased them. The artists believe that people degenerate and die in part because they live in spaces that are too comfortable. They designed abodes that cause people to be disoriented, challenged, and uncomfortable. The unusual features, such as sloping, bumpy floors, windows near the ceiling, and no inside doors should, according to the designers, stimulate the body and mind, thus prolonging life. Unfortunately they lost their life savings to Bernard Madoff, recently jailed because of multi-billion-dollar fraud (Efrate 2009).

Uncomfortable homes are not recommended, but when we circulate in the same group of friends who are exactly like us, there is no challenge or growth. The ability to leave our social comfort zones and risk meeting persons of other cultures, other financial circumstances, other educational levels, or other occupations, can embellish our perspectives on life. It requires a conscious effort, perhaps even some risk. Resources for such challenges are more likely to be available and changes are easier to initiate in midlife. So, do it now!

It is all too easy and comfortable for a retiree to take on a consumer role. All too often a virtual replacement for a real person becomes a partner. A person isolates himself or herself in the media masses and loses social functions, diminishing the meaning of life. Most modern information transmissions are not focused on the needs of individuals; they focus on standardized, commercialized use.

In aging individuals, it should be clear that with increasing age, vulnerability can increase with each change, be it physiological or social. Learning about intellectual functions and how to prevent hardening of the cerebral vascular net and decline of the intellect from the passive constant exposure to the mass media will ensure better preparation for aging. All types of activity that encourage a positive attitude, whether connected to previous employment or not, can slow decline. Even light physical activity has a positive influence on health in general and protection for heart disease. To maintain a desirable quality of life, increased life expectancy demands that we remain intellectually and physically fit.

Increased education often leads to activities that require further development. Especially fulfilling are hobbies that showed talent early in life such as music, painting, or writing. These types of hobbies carried over to late life may reawaken many memories. Hobbies can serve as a continuum of career, or as compensation for a career. There are many possibilities for developing new hobbies in late life, or to relearn one that was started earlier. Such development can play an important role in preventing loneliness and isolation. Clubs and facilities that offer activities and opportunities to learn and to meet new people are conducive to good health. However, involvement must not be forced, but must come from the love of relearning an old hobby or of learning a new one. It is ideal when a new activity has been started while still employed and can be taken up again in retirement.

Personal growth, whether through education or a new hobby or job, is more meaningful than killing time. Striving for self-fulfillment and self-development provides hope that a fresh fulfillment of life will lead to better and deeper meaning, and this provides another means for social integration.

The Terman studies were longitudinal studies of gifted children that began in 1921. The results of tests of the remaining eleven adults (still living at ages of 72–83), showed no intellectual deterioration. Not one of the eleven had fully retired. It appears as if they felt that ongoing intellectual activity produced a hormone elixir that kept them young. Through such activity, if one were to use talent and remain intellectually active, life could be prolonged by a decade; otherwise life could end prematurely (Schneidman 1989).

The importance of work to the older generation is obvious in the Terman studies. The surviving participants continued doing some kind of work. They did not capitulate to the myths of aging, and even in the very late decades, continued to live fully. The high correlation of mental and physical health with meaningful and fulfilling work is well established. One is never completely finished with a task as long as the strength remains to work. This is certainly a fact that the Terman studies successfully verified. Working to complete a goal or to fulfill a passion can be beneficial in late life. Perhaps this promoted their longevity.

Infectious diseases can influence one's entire life. Inoculation and other preventive measures should be taken. Prevention and timely recognition of illness is far more desirable than coping with chronic illness. A thorough check-up and compliance with recommendations can attenuate or prevent complications. Regular medical check-ups should begin no later than age forty.

Knowledge of proper nutrition is vitally important, as is following a plan of reducing calorie intake as one's energy requirements decline. One should not wait until the first alarm signals that corrections are needed. Being overweight, for example, is especially bad for the heart, the circulatory and respiratory systems, and even for the brain. Entering late life with excess baggage of any sort can cause adjustment to lower metabolic rates to be much more difficult. It is vitally important to be selective about what is consumed. Lowered metabolism demands more nutrient-dense instead of calorie-dense foods. I remember when my California physician told me to forget cheese. He explained that, as we age, we need more bulk, more fiber, and less fat. Funny, I don't miss cheese, and I only purchase it during special holidays, enjoying low-fat cheese in small amounts.

However, for many people over sixty-five, beginning new activities can be especially stressful. The risk associated with new experiences and new adventures may not appear worthwhile or relevant. Sometimes, in some socioeconomic levels, an older person seeking improvement has a lower status among peers! In America, many older people had to leave school very early in their education and many never learned to correctly read and write and to do simple calculations. Yet, these abilities are absolutely necessary in our advanced technological society. Older persons lacking basic education can experience an enormous increase of self-esteem when empowered to write, read, and calculate. Many others who are more educated have not used their abilities in a very long time. They grew up in a time when aging was seen as negative and when many negative stereotypes existed. However, learning in advanced age plays a strategic role for helping older people fulfill various needs, and at the same time, intellectual growth adds meaning to life. The possibilities of finding new friendships with like-minded persons is an important aspect of continued growth experiences. Longer life expectancies and better life-long education give many older adults a chance to enhance personal growth.

Just how long there will be enough money to finance extended years of life is a genuine concern of older adults. Savings plans should continue and be supplemented even in later life. Savings can be invested, long-term health care insurance and additional income sources can be considered. Most older adults are financially illiterate and do not know how to plan savings to last for many decades of life. Inflation and unemployment cause additional concerns because the purchasing power of their retirement incomes, and the financial stability of their insurance programs are endangered. Because of divorce or widowhood, training for a second career or development of an existing career may be necessary.

Empirical research confirms the views of the late Congressman Claude Pepper. He believed that the challenge is to recognize the vast experience, knowledge, and ability older people have to offer, and to learn how to develop the mechanism that uses these great resources.

In a speech, psychologist John Gardner spoke on the topic of personal renewal in later years. He said:

You have to build meaning into your life and you build it through your commitments—whether to your religion, to your loved ones, to your life work, to your fellow humans, to your conception of an ethical order. (1986, June 13)

Gardner continues by saying we can build this meaning out of our past, our affections and loyalties, out of our experiences, or out of our values.

Older adults want and need to volunteer. In a program called Senior Friendship Days in Palo Alto, California and in Savannah, Georgia, empowered volunteers reported that:

1. They did not feel lonesome;
2. They were convinced that their work was very important; and
3. They felt that volunteering benefits exceeded expectations.

Stimulation derived by participants in community activities contribute a certain feeling of power from helping with ongoing increasing social and economic problems. Empowered volunteers in the Savannah program reported that they felt no isolation. When they were administered the Life Attitude Profile (LAP), they showed increased self-esteem, better cardiovascular health, a greater number of friends, more frequent phone calls about their conditions, rides to the doctor by neighbors, and improved quality of life. This program became the standard model throughout area community centers and churches. The program continues to thrive at locations where it began.

What volunteers immediately seemed to sense is that interdependence as we age is logical. We need each other more; it is necessary for survival. Independence is a pipe dream in a world that is increasingly complex, and one in which interconnectedness is essential. If you doubt this, remember how helpless you feel when the electricity is interrupted, or when a tornado looms on the horizon. Gone are the days of the log cabin, the garden and the farmyard, when independence seemed feasible. Interdependence, in turn, demands a kind of resilience on the part of the individual and an evolving appropriate behavior. It calls for a supple mind and an openness to potentialities. Cicero said centuries ago that "We are so created that there exists a certain tie which strengthens our proximity to each other." It is adaptive to form new relationships as we lose old ones, and to accept interdependence as beneficial.

Often, simply from the joy of learning to learn, we become engaged with others in community activities. Classic works of literature, art, and music of the past have relevance to older adults and to the environment in which they live. Learning is so important because it can free older adults from the stereotypes of society that otherwise limit them. The search for knowledge can liberate one from withdrawal and release one to a new role in society. Through this, changes can occur that lead to more integration into society, with an accompanying feeling of power and ability to resolve conflicts. Memories can call forth knowledge and wisdom. It is a special gift of late life when one can look back and gain self understanding through one's contributions and mistakes, and can still set new priorities. After life review, a preview of what an older adult wishes for the remaining years can be motivating. Goethe concluded that *"Der Mensch ist am gluck-lichsten, der den Zusammenhange zwischen dem Anfang und dem Ende seines Lebens erkennt."* (One is happiest when one can see the connection between the beginning and the end of life).

Strength in the last phase of life is sometimes attributed to wisdom. Wisdom describes the ability to give life meaning and to live fully. It is not a universal trait unique to older adults; many young adults figure out life before they grow old! One has been described as wise when one has continued to learn throughout life, and through this, has built deeper insights of understanding and judgment. Through lifelong experiences, a person can learn to differentiate between the important and the irrelevant, easing problem solving and making crisis situations easier to overcome. Sometimes this means that problem solving isn't active, as a younger person would like, but rather a more passive acceptance. This results from insight in the limits and finality of life and from the acceptance that it is often simply not within our power to change some things. The solution may be to accept and to tolerate. The oft-quoted serenity prayer says it best:

God grant me the serenity
To accept the things I cannot change;
Courage to change the things I can;
And wisdom to know the difference.

The primary motivations for older persons to learn are joy, self-exploration, and connections in the community. The Elderhostel program is a good example: it combines travel, education, and friendship. It provides opportunities to widen one's horizons, to learn others perspectives on life, and to achieve insight and knowledge. However, one must make a strong effort to maintain physical and intellectual growth and to integrate oneself in the environment. Learning more about life's context through involvement in geographical, historical, and intellectual interests and activities creates enthusiasm.

Older adults who search for fulfillment and continue to educate themselves serve a subtle but very important role as good examples for others. They help lower anxiety about aging because they represent aging directly and show that the aging process can be improved through additional learning and preparation. By their example, they show that within there are "more resources of energy than have ever been tapped, more talent than has ever been exploited, more strength than has ever been tested, more to give than you have ever given" (Gardner 1990, 9). Continuing to learn is a must if one desires to be fulfilled and as happy as possible in late life.

If expectations for retirement are realistic, a person will more likely feel successful in the final stage of life. Aging will be viewed as an ongoing process of change and not as stagnation, a process in which one develops personality, remains active, and can retain rationality, self-confidence, and fulfillment. Through the use of total knowledge, experience, and abilities, one can be fulfilled. Or, so to say, *"Die Ernte des gelebten Lebens einbringen"* (to bring in the harvest of the full life). If such a person has lived intensively, accepted his whole life (as the best that one could do under the circumstances) and used his intellectual abilities, the result should be social and psychological fitness. Sitzmann suggests the following learning goals: to develop the ability to include/integrate others in life; the ability to maintain independence; and the ability to continue participation (1981). Other experts add to his suggestions: social competence, productivity, and happiness.

Attitude and happiness play a major role in how we age. Holahan (Holahan et al. 2008) studied happiness of persons ages sixty-six to eighty-six. He reported the results from 717 Terman study participants. They were asked to rate at age sixty-one their feelings about happiness. At later ages, sixty-six to eighty-six, a slight decline in happiness was reported. Overall, however, the large majority reported that they were "pretty happy" or "very happy" at advanced ages. Holahan also addressed positive expectancies about aging. Positive attitudes and positive thinking led to a higher quality of life and subsequently better adjustments. Educating individuals about successful aging may itself promote well-being far into the aging years.

As the population swells over the next decades, more and more of the nation's planners will have to focus on the needs of older adults. Learning about aging can prove helpful, not only to those who are aging, but also to many professionals, whether in health care, social work, engineering, or business.

Gaining an understanding of the aging process should be valuable to engineers, for example, who will be creating or redesigning products specifically for the elderly; to advertising and marketing managers who need to promote these products; to real-estate developers trying to build appropriate housing; to psychologists and health care workers who will be seeing more elderly clients, and to other professionals.

People working in golden age centers, senior centers, agencies on aging, retirement facilities, nursing homes, senior programs, and others having daily contact with senior adults should be required and obligated to learn more about aging issues (Garrett 1992). Retirees have the greatest responsibility to learn about the inevitability of changes and adjustments that late life brings. It is never too late to grow up; denial of aging is an immature, shortsighted approach to late life.

Release from life and from beloved people, as well as the departure from this earth, is easier when one can face the power of death without anxiety and doubt. When one lives the rest of life with full peaceful serenity and composure, he or she is seen as one with the universe and feels metaphysical support. Whoever reaches this stage and succeeds in being wise will be able to complete life, predominantly through the power of one's beliefs and acceptance. The final movement of the symphony of life will have been achieved.

eleven

FROM FASHION
TO PASSION

"Choose a job you love, and you will never have
to work a day in your life."

Studs Terkel

Too much of my life has been spent on looking good. Very vulnerable to the wishes of the men in my life, for one reason or another, I was influenced by several. Many women are stronger; they know who they are and they are not easily influenced. But, on my way to finding something about which I was passionate, with the empty nest and remarriage came a focus on maintaining my physical appearance. That wasn't all bad, because it drove my motivation to stay slim, thus avoiding obesity and the myriad of problems that result from excessive weight.

The first highly influential man in my life was my father. He fathered nine children, four of whom were pretty women. He loved seeing us dressed for Sunday church, and without doubt, I was his favorite. I was the spitting image of his wife, and although of opposite personalities from my mother, he admired my appearance, but he used to tell me that I needed more fat "to look more like a woman." When the first local beauty contest was implemented in Carthage, Tennessee, he enrolled three of his daughters as participants. Although I was ill the night of the pageant, I was not too ill to comply with his wishes. At the mid-pageant break, he was elected the "ugliest man," confirming his local popularity. At the end of the pageant, his favorite daughter became "Miss Smith County." That launched an overdose of self-esteem, especially with my sisters, who were shorter and tinier in frame, and around whom I felt clumsy because I was tall and weighed 117, unlike their 100–110.

I left Smith County and spent my first college semester at Tennessee Tech in Cookeville, about thirty miles from home. Naïve and inexperienced, having never traveled outside Tennessee, I still did not understand the power that comes with attractiveness. As a freshman, many of us attended the election of officers within a few weeks of my entrance in college. I was nominated for an office, as were four other females. I never knew who nominated me because I didn't know anyone yet. However, the five of us qualified by walking across the stage and guess who got the most applause! From then on, I questioned the judgment of the audience. I didn't last long at that college; an injury from a bad car accident terminated my first attempt to get a college education. Fast forward to age fifty and the many experiences that led me from my emphasis on fashion and attractiveness to something much more valuable.

I married a physician not too long after the accident. I was still searching for an identity and knowing his wonderful parents weighted my decision to marry him. His father had been my dentist all my life, and was the kindest man I had ever met. His mother, although I loved her much, was somewhat insecure intellectually and focused heavily on being very well dressed. She dressed me like a fashion model, and took great pride in so doing. Clothes and my appearance continued to matter a lot to her. Fortunately, she continued that with my daughter, and created intricately detailed little girl's dresses.

With the death of the first marriage twenty years later, I found that being single was not a bad thing. I was in total control, and I wanted to go back to school; I wanted to learn.

I was overwhelmed with responsibility for the children, house and yard maintenance, part-time work, and traveling from Savannah, Georgia to Georgia Southern and the University of Georgia at Athens for my first master's degree. I had been noticed by a bachelor, who encouraged me to fulfill my wish to go back to school. We were married three years later, after we met on the ski slopes in Germany. We made shopping trips, during which he spent way too much money on clothes for me. I fell for it! After we were married, he wanted to change my imperfect body—the shape, the toes, the eyes. I went along with fake eyelashes and toe surgery, and then began to rebel. My mother had drilled into all her girls that "pretty is as pretty does," and that refrain had influenced me as much as had the important men in my life. Still, it took a long time to gain the self-confidence that appearance was not the most important thing in my life, and my new husband conformed to my wishes.

I changed my focus, and gave up looking for the fountain of youth sometime during the fifth decade of my life. I was a late bloomer, and having spent most of the previous half-century of my life with family concerns and with educational opportunities (when inexpensive and available), I achieved full-time work for the first time at age fifty. In the next quarter of a century, I began the search for a passion, because unlike Ponce de Leon, I knew that the search for a fountain of youth was to be found in something beyond self, not somewhere in Florida.

I had studied aging issues for several decades, and I was sure that my passion would be expressed somehow in the field of aging. My first part-time job in aging was with the Santa Clara County Educational System in Palo Alto, and with it came the realization that my destiny was being created. In Palo Alto, I convinced the community center director that we could attract older adults with a program I was planning. He emphatically asserted that nothing would attract seniors. I asked only for the opportunity to show that seniors would vote with their feet; if the program were fulfilling and if it met their needs, they would attend. The director and staff reluctantly agreed to set up for fifty seniors.

Five hundred people entered the program the first day, and the crowds grew exponentially within a year. Feeding the crowd was the greatest challenge on opening day, but the staff was fully cooperative, and they scurried to purchase and serve food. Seniors like crafts, practical and relevant new knowledge, food, music, dance and, most of all, camaraderie and opportunities to contribute their talents, to help each other, and to be appreciated. They want to be connected and to contribute to the community, and most of all they want someone to listen. All this and more was provided. It was demanding because of the rapid growth of dozens of volunteers. To retain a staff of volunteers, ongoing appreciation and recognition of their efforts was the trick—they just kept coming. It was immensely rewarding.

I discovered that once self-esteem is restored, most older adults forget about their chronological age and think only of functional age. The bottom line being, "If I think I can, I can." Without victim blaming, I sincerely believe that most of us in later life are much more capable than we credit ourselves.

A year later, in near-death condition at Stanford Hospital (nurse's error) as I awaited a doctor, I noticed that it was 2 PM. I focused on what the seniors would be doing in my program at that time of day—they would be listening to speakers from nearby Stanford on subjects the seniors had requested, followed by the Grand March and several folk dances that I had taught them. That vision was both distracting and comforting. It was comforting to me that many older adults were enjoying a happy quality of life at that moment as a result of their involvement with each other, and their belief that they were valued. I really thought that I was dying and it was rewarding to know that at least I would leave a connected community of seniors who could help each other. The doctor arrived and told the negligent nurse that she had given me an overdose of morphine (for pain following surgery). I slowly stopped rising off the bed (as if my entire body were in a spasm) and collapsing back onto it.

After establishing programs for the mature crowd in Palo Alto, I understood what is and what isn't effective when working with older adults. I had studied andragogy (the accepted method/philosophy of older adult education), but I felt that older adults needed a different philosophy and different ways of expressing themselves. I created what I felt was education with meaning, and I labeled it "logogogy" (*logos* is the Greek word for "meaning"). I set out to enhance self-efficacy in older adults and to provide programs for them which would add meaning to their lives.

After three years of directing Palo Alto programs, we returned to our former home in Savannah, Georgia. I implemented the same program there for the Chatham County Board of Education, the City Recreational Department, and Senior Citizens, Inc. This provided a three-legged stool to ensure that if funding were cut at one agency, the seniors would not be disappointed.

I did not want to be a part of something that would bring disappointment to seniors, and expectations that we would not be able to deliver. Within three years, the programs spread from one neighborhood to another, housed in various churches. I had to slow down the tapes I used for exercise and rhythms, but the southern seniors gradually increased in strength and ability. The Savannah program lasted seven years before the board of education in Chatham reduced its budget. There was no money for older folks because the illiteracy rate was so high among students. Funding was diverted to eradicate the high illiteracy rate of the K–12 students. I explained to my posse of volunteers that they had senior power, and that the younger folks needed to improve their reading, writing, and arithmetic. The seniors themselves could take over the senior program; they did, and they are still doing it!

In fact, shortly before this happened they had shown up in large numbers for the first Mrs. Senior Savannah contest. I had not entered the contest because I was buried with work with my full-time job and evening teaching at both local branches of the University of Georgia. The senior center director, Al Henderson, called me at work and asked me to join the first contest, because he was concerned that there wouldn't be enough competition to hold it. Al was one of my best supporters (one of the three-legged stool I had used to keep my program operating in case an agency cut back its funding) in the senior endeavors. I told him that I was too busy and did not have time to drive downtown to register. Shortly after the phone call, a senior center employee approached my office with a request to sign the application to enter the contest. What else could I do but participate! Actually, I enjoyed it, and when I walked on stage for the first round, the audience was packed with my seniors. I said to myself, *I must win this; I owe it to them!* The next day at work during the lunchtime program, one volunteer approached me with an envelope. The seniors had collected three hundred dollars to give me to buy a dress for the contest when I was in Washington. I was embarrassed and overwhelmed with emotion. I had planned a trip to the American Society on Aging the next week and while there, I found a consignment shop and bought a dress for three hundred dollars. It was from the shop where the senators' wives sold their dresses after they had worn them once. I found a seven hundred fifty dollar original dress for exactly three hundred. I not only wore the dress with the intentions of winning for my flock, I made another side trip to have the total confidence that I would win. I had noticed that the other nine contestants had long, beautifully manicured fingernails. My gardening hands suffered from work in the yard, plus some nail biting. On the way to the final event, I asked my husband to stop and hold the car while I went into Walmart. I quickly purchased a package of artificial nails, rushed back to the car, and applied them on the way to the finals. It must have been the nails and the lovingly-donated dress, I thought, as I was crowned in front of all of my seniors, the first Mrs. Senior Savannah. The bad news came later; I couldn't remove the nails. It took six weeks for my nails to appear normal again—worn and short.

The seniors' program had expanded so rapidly that I needed help from people trained in gerontology. I had already gone to the local universities to teach gerontology in the evenings at the local branches of the University of Georgia and at Georgia Southern University. I had connected the students there with the wellness programs that I had piloted. Three days after the senior program lost funding, I was hired to teach full-time at the local extension of the University of Georgia, Armstrong Atlantic State University. This time in my life was extremely enjoyable, and I sometimes regretted that I retired from that experience after a decade.

Moving on to Nashville, where my grandchildren lived, I was confronted with unexpected challenges from many directions. Hoping to just hang out in the nine acres of pristine forest and the lovely home we had purchased, I stayed alert by writing newspaper articles. I was soon discovered via the articles and was invited to speak at the historic Maxwell House. This opportunity netted a job offer, which was not my objective. The next day I visited the local Area Agency on Aging and Disability (AAAD).

The first senior exposition wellness fair was being planned in Nashville at Greater Nashville's AAAD. I refused to get heavily involved until I discovered a real need for my abilities. I agreed to work part time, because if the first senior expo wellness fair was successful, seniors would vote with their feet each year at an annual event. Hundreds of seniors attended the first expo, and the numbers greatly increased over the next eight years.

Immediately following the first expo, I was called by Meharry Medical College to work at the only geriatric education center in Tennessee. My husband, whom I had trained at the master's level at the Georgia university, replaced me at the AAAD, and I joined forces with Meharry for ten hours a week. Within a month, I was offered the position of Director of the Center on Aging. My response to the chair of internal medicine: "But I am not qualified; I am a professor, not an administrator!" He liked the response; I was hired. Thus ended my search for a passion; it was being laid out for me.

I had to write my first grant to get funding for the program at the medical college. After a month of grant writing with much help from Dr. Maciej Buchowski and several days of around-the-clock preparation, my husband and I left for Montana on a business vacation. There were no funds for the Geriatric Education Consortium unless I was awarded a grant. Two weeks after driving west across country, we received a phone call from Nashville: two million dollars had been awarded from the feds. Returning home, I was now able to implement what I had designed in the grant application. I was energized at a level I had never experienced before!

Shortly afterward, I was invited to lecture to health professionals in the area and to medical students. Getting health profession personnel interested in aging topics was a real challenge. I established a Medical Gerontology Certificate Program based on the one that I had taught in Georgia. For a fee of twenty-five dollars, subsidized by grant money, health personnel of all educational and skill levels could attend three Fridays of training on aging issues. Within five years, we had trained sixteen thousand professionals and para-professionals.

My first attempt toward motivating medical students to learn about aging issues was to establish the Geriatric Student Forum (GSF). Young, first-year medical students listened; they were not yet concerned about paying back debts and establishing a practice. Fully aware that African Americans prefer a minority physician, I sensed an urgency to prepare young

African Americans to serve the increasing numbers of older minorities! I enjoyed teaching and I soon learned to love the students; in fact, I became passionate about my job. I spent a rewarding time annually with student leaders, such as Dr. Monica Garbutt-Anselmetti, first president of the GSF who is now a successful doctor in Olympia, Washington. There were several unforgettable leaders of the student club during the decade I worked with them; another was Dr. Samuel Williams, now a successful resident in Internal Medicine at Boston University Hospital. Sam provided excellent leadership to the forum, after the previous student president was removed from her duties by the dean. Sam revived the student forum and never neglected his duty as president. For example, as I had requested, he was standing on the street in front of the West Basic Science Building at Meharry when I arrived in my car with Dr. Walter Bortz to address the students about the future of geriatrics. Sam had filled the lecture hall with students, directed delivery of food for the forum students, and waited for me outside the medical complex to escort Bortz to the podium.

Bortz had returned to Meharry for a second time after presenting to large crowds of professionals two years earlier. Always willing to accommodate the agenda created for him, he would address varied groups: Grand Rounds with Vanderbilt University and at Meharry; the Tennessee Vulnerable Adult Coalition; Vanderbilt residents in internal medicine; and then at his request, a private dinner with my friends.

After three days of numerous speaking engagements, I took Walter to Hendersonville, and we walked in our private forest for an hour before dinner, arriving back at my house just in the nick of time to meet the guests. Thankful that my husband had dinner under control, conversation focused on the rock formations from the Ice Ages we had just seen in the forest, and Bortz' concern about huge cedar trees that had been chopped down by a neighbor. Guests included the county judge and some physicians I thought Walter would enjoy meeting.

My passion (and grant money) to educate minority doctors and medical students about aging led me to invite nationally known speakers to talk with them. A sample of speakers included: Leonard Hayflick, PhD, San Francisco University; Monsignor Charles Fahey, Fordham University; Harry Moody, PhD, The Longevity Institute; Michael Helgeson, DDS, founder of Appletree Dentistry; Eric Hardt, MD, Boston University; Conrad Nau, MD, West Virginia University; Paul Rubens, MD, Johns Hopkins University; Walter Bortz II, MD,

Stanford University; Marie Bernard, MD, National Institute on Aging, and others. All were enthusiastically received by students and faculty.

Dental students were also included in aging issues because as I aged, I realized how important dentition is for good nutrition. I wanted old folks to keep their teeth as they aged, and educating future dentists was a link toward accomplishing that. The Dean of the School of Dentistry was pleased to join my efforts. Dental students became active in the GSF, and the Dean of Public Health, with impressive geriatric credentials, also lectured in aging studies.

Studs Terkel had remarked that if you can "Find a job you love, you'll never have to work a day in your life." I had found that job. Although there were many challenges, the rewards of working with the students kept me on a ten-year high. I realized that I was growing younger as I became interested in the lives of the students. That's what kept me trucking—caring for, loving others, and being mentally challenged. The students were actually adding days to my life. I would recall what I had read about how researchers had documented increases in hours and days of lives of their pets, simply by caring for them differently. Pets that had been picked up and loved as they were fed had much stronger hearts and far fewer clogged arteries.

My pleasure in working with the students, and their return of respect and cooperation must have improved my cardiovascular health because my energy level kept pace with theirs. Caring for others not only adds years to our lives, it adds life to our years.

Anonymity in a historically black college for a white, silver-haired septuagenarian was impossible. Most faculty and many students greeted me by name. I became bolder and approached faculty about sending students to visit senior wellness centers instead of nursing homes and the veterans hospitals, their prior routine. Faculty member, Dr. Susan Deriemer, shared my enthusiasm and we were soon allowed to schedule second-year students for annual screenings of healthy seniors at our senior wellness fair. Seniors really liked the students. Our screening booth was the busiest of the 110 booths at the second senior expo. I later began to schedule students for interviews in assisted living homes and senior centers. The visits to interview healthy older adults were positively evaluated by both students and seniors. I have included some of the many responses from the students after their training in the Growth Development and Aging (GDA) Course and after their older adult interviews:

What did you learn in the course that will help you in your future practice as physicians?

• "The geriatrics section of this course is leaps and bounds above any other section. I felt like I was actually prepared for the site visit and for the exam."

• "Yes, I found the geriatrics section useful—it gave information on how to treat this population that we had not previously received."

• "I believe seeing the more positive aspects of geriatrics is the most important because the majority of students are used to seeing only the negative."

• "I found the geriatrics section useful because (as much as I do not like admitting it) I was one of the people who stereotyped seniors. It was very interesting because it gave us new experiences."

• "I felt the geriatrics course was useful because there were a lot of things that I did not put into perspective. For example, the part that aging does occur, but it does not have to occur the way it does. If people stay healthy, then they do not have to worry about growing old."

• "Thank God for this course, Drs. DeReimer and Garrett. The geriatrics session was good because there was a senior citizen teaching us, so she had personal experiences."

• "The geriatrics section was well done. It definitely made me more interested in treating elderly patients— no improvement needed."

• "This was a useful section because I did not know much about the older population. I did not know that elder abuse was common, so now that I know the signs I can determine if someone is being abused."

• "Dr. Garrett made good points about not prescribing medications for elderly people, but prescribing preventive treatments, so they can live healthy and independent lives. This section exposed me to both the harsh and the encouraging realities about the elderly population."

• "Exposing us to the issues the elderly face was great. Dr. Garrett presents very interesting material, and she did so in a very lively manner."

Here are a few of the many responses to onsite visit interviews with older adults:

Did you find the observation and interview experience useful? Why or why not?

• "Actually, out of all the observations in this course, the best one actually has me thinking of going into geriatrics! I got to see a new side of being older, a healthier active side, instead of the dying, sad, and mean people side."

• "Being active is the key. I can't believe that this woman was ninety-five. And she was still moving around!"

• "This experience has opened my eyes to new possibilities for my future as a senior citizen. I never imagined that life could be so grand and of such high quality for people over seventy."

• "The atmosphere was very warm and welcoming and seeing the relatively great shape that the ninety-two year old was in, I definitely plan on taking much better care of my mind, body, and soul—starting today. When I grow up, I wanna be just like her!"

• "Usually when I think of someone who is eighty-nine years old, I do not picture them walking around without difficulties, without using a walker or cane. I usually picture them in a nursing home under constant medical care. This experience showed me that this is not necessarily the case. If you take care of your body, then it will be in better condition when you get old."

• "This experience made me realize how I need to continue to be active. Seeing the senior in the exercise class who was ninety-five years old was amazing! One said that you must stay active in order to keep yourself healthy!"

• "I think that being around the seniors also allowed me to realize that getting old is not bad at all, and that I'm in control of my experience. I need to be sure that I remain healthy and to always go to my physician for my wellness visits so that I prevent disease instead of treating disease."

• "Respect is important. Especially when dealing with the older population. I think that physicians sometimes lose themselves in their authority. Every patient is a person, whose life experience affects their perspective on life. Each patient should be treated as an individual who wants the same thing out of life that we as physicians want. They want to live happy, healthy, and productive lives."

- "I learned about assisted living. I have always wondered what they were like. This information may be important in talking to patients who are thinking about placing loved ones in a nursing home, or other alternatives."

- "I learned not to prejudge my patients based on their age."

- "I learned that everyone wants to feel that they matter regardless of age. They want to feel important and to be listened to, something I will strive to do in my practice."

- "I must learn to adapt my way of communication with my patients according to their personalities, culture, and different age groups."

- "I learned that physical disabilities do not equate to mental disabilities."

- "Outside social interaction will decrease the incidence of depression and psychiatric diseases. Exercising will cut down on other illnesses and increase joint movement, which will cut down on arthritis. And, just being a companion will allow them to talk about their past experiences and let them know how valuable their life has been. This is extremely important and I hope all of my colleagues will join in my efforts!"

My teaching experience in medical school was really rewarding. Soon promoted to associate professor, lecturing four to nine times a year was a challenge. I was not a medical doctor, and addressing medical students and faculty (including Grand Rounds for the physicians) was especially challenging. I never pretended to know the clinical side of aging; I discussed what I knew from research, training, and from my own personal aging. The clinical part of training required a braver soul. When dissecting animals in a biology course as a freshman in college, I changed my mind about becoming a medical doctor.

The worst experience I had during this decade was with a Caucasian, menopausal geriatrician who requested assignment to the Geriatric Education Center (GEC). What a trouble maker she was! She marched in with folded arms and announced that she was now my boss and that I would do whatever she mandated. I put up with her demands for a while and then decided I could not do my work in her presence, so I submitted my resignation. The president, Dr. John Maupin, ran interference for me, sending me to Dean Coney, who was to place me wherever I wanted to move in the medical college. I didn't care that much; I just wanted to be free of this irate, troublesome geriatrician. Having operated for half a decade without a boss, and while paying my own salary with grant awards, I was really ready to resign. Instead, with the disturbing doctor out of sight, I would not give up what I enjoyed. I requested transfer of my grant and my work to the neurology department; their chair had been the most helpful with grant fulfillment during the previous five years. Within a few hours, I was assigned to neurology. The geriatrician was soon sent to manage a nursing home, and although I was happy to be rid of her, I felt sorry for the poor nursing home residents.

Working at Meharry was a challenge from day one. Many employees in the infrastructure of the administrative system had been doing the same job for decades. Understandably, monotonous routines led to inefficiencies and often defensive reactions, so I quickly learned by trial and error. I was responsible for federal funds, and as the program grew, I selected a Peruvian college graduate assistant who made my life easier and more productive for many years.

Despite administrative complications, the Meharry experience was unforgettable. Faculty and medical staff from all corners of the globe provided a good experience—East India, Poland, Nigeria, Latin America, Lebanon, China, Russia, Korea, and Singapore. The cultural environment was stimulating. It expanded my knowledge and provided opportunities to develop new relationships from many countries.

I will never forget the Nigerian student who rushed to my office for a visit. His former wife and his son were coming for his graduation. His girlfriend, his parents, grandparents, and uncle were also coming. The parents were divorced; the uncle would not speak to his brother, the student's father. His lovely mother had brought a new friend; the student was distraught with worry about how he could accommodate all of them at graduation. I advised him to carry the message to them that it was his day, and all of them must forget their animosities and make him proud. They did. I handed the student a card with a check as he passed in front of the faculty at graduation; my only regret was that my check was not larger because I believe this person is genuine and will serve patients well.

My grant reward included funds to distribute to the Geriatric Education Consortium (GEC). Affiliation with Vanderbilt's Internal Medicine Department was the easiest part of my job. Dr. James Powers was my best supporter during good and difficult times. A kind, intelligent geriatrician, he was my local role model and was always there when I needed advice.

There were many unforgettable positive experiences at Meharry. I met a student who told me that there were five living generations in her family. This was another indication that I had to help students understand how the demographic imperative would affect their future. The rapid increase in our older population, especially in the minority populations, will change health care demands. As the Caucasian population declines, it is urgent that we prepare for these demographic changes. The need for health professionals at every skill level is pressing, and we are far behind many countries in preparing for the boomer tsunami.

We must take advantage of every opportunity to increase the education of medical students, faculty, and the general population about the demographic changes around the globe, and how these changes will affect the delivery of health care. It is equally pressing that we continue to showcase those healthy seniors who portray what the pope said: "Aging should be the crown of life; it should bring in the harvest—the harvest of all that we have learned, experienced and accomplished. Like the last movement of a great symphony, the important themes of life should come together in one triumphant movement." Enjoy fashion, but to bring in the harvest, one needs a passion.

Writer Matthew Scully sums up this final statement beautifully in an article in the *International Journal of Logotherapy*. He wrote the article on September 4, 1997 about the death of Viktor Frankl. Many remember that Princess Diana's tragic accident occurred on August 31 of that same year. Although Scully also succumbed to the lure of Princess Di, as did most of us, the notice of Dr. Frankl's death was not mentioned anywhere assessable to most people.

I have wondered for years why I never heard anything about his final years. He had died at the age of ninety-two within hours of Lady Di's death. But, as Scully reported, the news of his passing was crowded out by the death of Princess Diana. Scully wrote, "Beauty will always draw a bigger crowd than wisdom . . . but perhaps we can interrupt our worship for just a moment to remember one of the truly great people of the century." Scully had interviewed Frankl in Vienna and quoted him as he stood beside a bust of Freud in his Vienna apartment. Frankl is quoted as saying that Freud's error was to forget the "upper stories—man as a creature of conscience and not just a bundle of appetites, drives and a lust for power" (1998, 32). Scully continued to discuss the timing of the deaths and reported that "probably he'd [Frankl] have diagnosed the events of [the] week as further evidence of an existential void." Scully closed his article by stating that it would be a safe bet that we would not see Frankl on the cover of *Time* or *People* . . . "but with his passing we should prize wisdom as much as beauty: We need it more, and it lasts a lot longer" (1998, 34).

— WORKS CITED —

Agostino, Joseph N. 1988. "Religiosity and Religious Participation in the Later Years: A Reflection of the Spiritual Needs of the Elderly." *Journal of Religious Gerontology.* Vol. 4. No. 2. (June), 75–82.

Altman, Paula. 1983. "Aptitude and Aging." *Higher Education Review.* Vol. 16. No. 1. California, 36–54.

Ansberry, Clare. 2009. "Elderly Emerge as a New Class of Workers—and the Jobless." *The Wall Street Journal,* (February 23).

Beauvoir, Simone de. 1970. *The Coming of Age.* New York: Éditions Gallimard.

Bianchi, Eugene C. 1982. *Aging as a Spiritual Journey.* New York: Crossroad.

Birren, James E. 1986. "The Process of Aging: Growing Up and Growing Old." *Our Aging Society: Paradox and Promise.* Eds. Alan Pifer and Lydia Bronte. New York: W. W. Norton & Co., 263–81.

Birren, James E. and Jayne Renner. 1980. "Concepts of Mental Health and Aging." *Handbook of Mental Health and Aging.* Eds. James E. Birren and R. Bruce Sloan. Englewood Cliffs, New Jersey: Prentice Hall, 3–33.

Blythe, Ronald. 1979. *The View in Winter: Reflections on Old Age.* New York: Harcourt Brace Jovanovich.

Borchert, Manfred and Karin Derichs-Kunstmann. 1982. *Neue Wege in der Altenbildung.* Konzept, Verlauf und Ergebnisse des Medienverbundprojektes. "Un-Ruhestand." Berlin.

Boron, Julie Blaskewicz, Nicholas A. Turiano, Sherry L. Willis, and K. Warner Schaie. 2007. "Effects of Cognitive Training on Change in Accuracy in Inductive Reasoning Ability." *The Journals of Gerontology Series B.* Psychological Sciences and Social Sciences.

Bortz, Walter M. II MD. 2007. *We Live Too Short and Die Too Long: How to Achieve and Enjoy Your Natural 100-Year Life Span.* New York: Select Books.

Bujard, Otker. 1982. "Trotz Fleiß kein Preis." *Unruhestand.* Eds. Manfred Borchert, Karin Derichs-Kunstmann, and Margret Hamann. Hamburg, 121–50.

Butler, Robert N. 1975. *Why Survive? Being Old in America.* New York: Harper & Row.

Cicero, Marcus Tullius. 1979. "De Senectute, De Amicitia, De Divinatione." *Cicero.* Trans. William Armistead Falconer. Massachusetts, 1–99.

Cohen, Donna. 1977. "An Exposition to the Concept of Lifelong Self-Education." *Educational Gerontology.* Vol. 2. No. 2. New York (April), 157–61.

Cohen, Gene D. 2005. *The Mature Mind: The Positive Power of the Aging Brain.* New York: Basic Books.

Cousins, Norman. 1979. *Anatomy of an Illness as Perceived by the Patient: Reflections on Healing and Regeneration.* New York: W. W. Norton & Co.

Curtin, Sharon. 1972. *Nobody Ever Died of Old Age.* Boston: Little Brown.

Doidge, Norman. 2007. *The Brain that Changes Itself: Stories of Personal Triumph from the Frontiers of Brain Science.* New York: Viking.

Dychtwald, Ken Phd. and Joe Flower. 1989. *The Age Wave: How the Most Important Trend of Our Time Can Change Your Future.* Los Angeles: J. P. Tarcher.

Dye, Celeste. 1980. "Autotelic Inquiry: An Approach to Attitude Change." *Educational Gerontology.* Vol. 5. No. 3. (July), 239–48.

Eadie, Betty J. with Curtis Taylor. 1992. *Embraced by the Light.* Placerville, CA: Gold Leaf Press.

Efrate, Amir. 2009. "Couples Dream of Immortality at Death's Door, Thanks to Madoff." *Wall Street Journal.* (March 24), A1.

Erikson, Erik H., Joan M. Erikson, and Helen Q. Kivnik. 1986. *Vital Involvement in Old Age.* New York: W. W. Norton & Co.

Fabry, Joseph B. 1968. *The Pursuit of Meaning: Viktor Frankl, Logotherapy, and Life.* San Francisco: Harper & Row.

Fisher, Lucy Rose. 1986. *Linked Lives: Adult Daughters and Their Mothers.* New York: Harper & Row.

Frankl, Viktor E. 1967. *Psychotherapy and Existentialism.* New York: Washington Square Press.

———. 1969. *The Will to Meaning: Foundations and Applications of Logotherapy.* New York: World Pub. Co.

———. 1978. *The Unheard Cry for Meaning: Psychotherapy and Humanism.* New York: Simon & Schuster.

———. 1984. *Man's Search for Meaning: An Introduction to Logotherapy.* New York: Simon & Schuster.

Freedman, Marc. 2007. *Encore: Finding Work that Matters in the Second Half of Life.* New York: Public Affairs.

Gaitz, Charles M. and Roy V. Varner. 1980. "Preventative Aspects of Mental Illness in Late Life." *Handbook of Mental Health and Aging.* Eds. James E. Birren and R. Bruce Sloane. New Jersey, 959–79.

Gardner, John. 1986. Commencement Address. Sidwell Friends School, Washington D. C. June 13. http://www.pbs.org/johngardner/sections/writings_speech_3.html. Accessed August 31, 2009.

———. 1990. "Personal Renewal." Delivered to McKinsey & Company. Phoenix, Arizona. November, 10. http://www.pbs.org/johngardner/sections/writings_speech_1.html. Accessed August 31, 2009.

Garrett, Ruth. 1991. *Alter-Schicksal oder Zeit der Fülle?: Lebenssituationen und Probleme älterer Menschen als gerontagogische Herausforderung.* Regensburg, Germany: S. Roderer.

————. 1992. "Retirement Doesn't Mean Getting Old." *Savannah Morning News* (September 12).

————. 1998. "Seniors Need to Get Motivated." *Savannah Morning News*. (February).

Goldberg, Sheldon. 1996. "Where Have Nursing Homes Been? Where Are They Going?" *Generations*. Vol 19. No. 4. California, 78–81.

Gonzales, Laurence. 2008. "Everyday Survival." *National Geographic Adventure*. (August).

Hamann, Bruno. 1988. *Familie heute*. Frankfurt.

Hohmeier, Jürgen. 1978. "Alter als Stigma." *Alter als Stigma*. Hohmeier, Jürgen. Frankfurt, 10–30.

Holahan, Carole K., Charles J. Holahan, Katherine E. Velasquez, and Rebecca J. North. 2008. "Longitudinal Change in Happiness during Aging: The Predictive Role of Positive Expectancies," *International Journal of Aging and Human Development*. Vol. 66. No. 3., 229–41.

Kimble, Melvin A. and James W. Ellor. 1989. "Logotherapy: An Overview." (Referat: Forum on Religion and Aging of the American Society of Aging. Washington, D. C. March 17, 1989). National College of Education. Evanston, Illinois, 1–10.

Knowles, Malcolm. 1974. *The Adult Learner*. Texas.

Kubler-Ross, Elisabeth. 1969. *On Death and Dying*. New York: Macmillan.

Kuczynski, Alex. 2006. *Beauty Junkies: Inside Our $15 Billion Obsession with Cosmetic Surgery*. New York: Doubleday.

Laube, Clifford J. 1980. "Up from Ageism." Media and Methods. Vol. 16. No. 6. Pennsylvania (February), 39–42.

Leaf, Alexander. 1973. "Every Day Is a Gift When You Are Over 100." *National Geographic* (January), 92–119.

Lehr, Ursula. 1984. *Psychologie des Alterns*. 5. Aufl. Heidelberg.

————. 1987. "Von der neuen Kunst des Älterwerdens." *Das neue Alter-Wie wollen wir morgen älter werden?* Bonn, 10–33.

Lesnoff-Caravaglia, Gari, ed. 1985. *Value, Ethics, and Aging*. New York: Human Sciences Press.

Lewis, Ivan A. 1989. "Elderly Are Happier, Poll Shows." *San Jose Mercury News* (May 4).

Maloney, Lawrence. 1983. "The Selling of Eternity." *Social Issues Resources.* Vol. 1. No. 84. Florida, 62–65.

McFadden, Susan. 2005. A paper from the University of Wisconsin Oshkosh distributed at the American Society on Aging Annual Convention.

Moody, Harry R. 1987. "Success in the Liberal Arts: A Tale of Two Programs," *Generations.* Vol. 2. No. 2. California (Winter), 59–60.

Moos, Rudolf H. and Jeanne A. Schaefer. 1986. *Coping with Life Crises: An Integrated Approach.* New York: Plenum Press.

Moramarch, Dheila. 1978. "Teach about Aging." *Learning.* Vol. 6. No. 7. New York, 44–46.

Olbrich, Erhard. 1986. "Coping in Old Age." *Age, Health, and Employment.* Eds. James E. Birren, Pauline K. Robinson, and Judy E. Livingston. Englewood Cliffs, New Jersey: Prentice-Hall, 45–62.

Pastolon, Leon. 1981. "Life Space over the Life Span." Journal of Housing. Vol. 4. No. 1. New York, 73–85.

Peck, Scott M. 1978. *The Road Less Traveled: A New Psychology of Love, Traditional Values, and Spiritual Growth.* New York: Simon & Schuster.

Percival, Harold Waldwin. 1946. *Thinking and Destiny.* New York: The New World Foundation.

Peterson, James A. 1980. "Social-Psychological Aspects of Death and Dying." *Handbook of Mental Health and Aging.* James E. Birren and R. Bruce Sloane. New Jersey.

Pifer, Alan. 1986. "The Public Policy Response." *Our Aging Society: Paradox and Promise.* Eds. Alan Pifer and Lydia Bronte. New York: W. W. Norton & Co., 391-414.

Ramsey, Janet L. 2007. "Learning from *Everyman*: Thoughts on Spirituality, Love, and Death in the Lives of Older Couples," *Generations.* Vol. 31. No. 3., 57–59.

Reker, Gary and Kerry Chamberlain, eds. 2000. *Exploring Existential Meaning: Optimizing Human Development Across the Life Span.* Thousand Oaks, CA: Sage Publications.

Robbins, John. 2007. *Healthy at 100: The Scientifically Proven Secrets of the World's Healthiest and Longest-lived Peoples.* New York: Ballantine Books.

Rosenmayr, Hilde and Leopold Rosenmayr. 1983. "Gesellschaft, Familie, Alternsprozeß." *Das Alter.* Reimann, Helga/Horst Reimann. Stuttgart, p. 45–69.

Rosenmayr, Leopold. 1981. "Alters vorbereitung-ein Weg zu sich selbst?" Pro Senectute. Zürich, 17–38.

———. 1983. *Die späte Freiheit.* Das Alter-ein Stück bewußt gelebten Lebens. Berlin.

Roth, Phillip. 2007. *Everyman.* Boston: Houghton Mifflin.

Schneider, Hans-Dietrich. 1981. "Selbstverständnis, Ziele, Inhalte und Formen der Vorbereitung auf das Alter." *Vorbereitung auf das Alter im Lebenslauf: Beiträge aus Theorie und Praxis.* Pro Senectute. Paderborn. u. a, 39–61.

———. 1983. "Wie lässt sich die Motivation zur Altersvorbereitung erhöhen?" *Archiv für Wissenschaft und Praxis der sozialen Arbeit.* 14. Jg., 147–55.

Schneider, John. 1984. Stress, Loss, and Grief: Understanding Their Origins and Growth Potential. Baltimore: University Park Press.

Schneidman, Edwin. 1989. "The Indian Summer of Life: A Preliminary Study of Septuagenarians." *American Psychologist.* Vol. 44. No. 4, 684–94.

Scott-Maxwell, Florida. 1968. *The Measure of My Days.* New York: Knopf.

Scully, Matthew. 1998. "Facing Our Fate without Flinching." *International Journal of Logotherapy.* Vienna. Vol. 6. No. 1. Spring.

Seitelberger, Franz. 1982. "Das Altern-Ein Entwicklungsgeschehen." *Aspekte des Menschlichen Alterns.* Österreichische Akademie der Wissenschaften. Wien, 7–19

Sheehy, Gail. 1976. *Passages: Predictable Crises of Adult Life.* New York: Dutton.

Sitzmann, Gerhard Helmut. 1981. "Die Organisation der Vorbereitung auf das Alter als pädagogisches Problem." *Die ältere Generation.* Braun, Walter. Bad Heilbrunn, 113–36.

Skinner, B. F. 1983. *Enjoy Old Age: A Program of Self-Management.* New York: Norton.

Soudek, Ingrid H. 1979. "Waiting for the End." in *The Pharos of Alpha Omega Alpha: Social Issues Resources Series.* Vol. 42. No. 3. Florida.

Stackelberg, Lorenz V. 1985. "Immer weniger Deutsche wollen uralt werden." *Mangfall Bote.* Donnerstag. Bad Aibling. No. 252. (October).

Stearns, Ann Kaiser. 1986. "How to Live through Loss." *Reader's Digest.* Vol. 129. No. 771. New York, 16–18.

Teague, Michael L., David M. Rosenthal, Valerie L. McGhee, and David Kearns. 1997. *Health Promotion: Achieving High-Level Wellness in the Later Years.* Madison, WI: Brown & Benchmark.

Tews, Hans Peter. 1979. *Soziologie des Alterns.* 3. Aufl. Heidelberg.

Thomae, Hans. 1980. "Personality and Adjustment to Aging." *Handbook of Mental Health and Aging.* Eds. James E. Birren and R. Bruce Sloane. New Jersey, 285–309.

———. 1983. *Alternsstile und Altersschicksale: ein Beitrag zur differentiellen Gerontologie.* Bern, Germany: H. Huber.

Tibbits, Clark. 1979. "Can We Invalidate Negative Stereotypes of Aging." *Gerontologist.* Vol. 19. No. 1. Washington (February), 10–20.

Tombs, David A. 1984. *Growing Old: A Handbook for You and Your Aging Parent.* New York: Viking Press.

Tournier, Paul. 1972. *Learn to Grow Old.* New York: Harper & Row.

———. 1978. *Die Chance des Alters.* Bern.

Trauth, John and Alan Bernstein. 2007. "Intelligent Retirement Planning: It's about More than Money." *Aging Today.* Vol. 28. No. 4. (July).

U.S. Bureau of the Census. 2005. *Distribution of Women 40 to 44 Years Old by Number of Children Ever Born and Marital Status: Selected years, 1970 to 2004* from http://www.census.gov/population/socdemo/fertility/tabH2.xls (accessed May 21, 2009).

Wang, Xiao Yan. 2008. "China to Shift Focus to Aging in Place." *Aging Today.* Vol. 29. No. 4. (July), 8.

Washington, D. C. Federal Interagency Forum on Aging-Related Statistics. *2006 Older American Update: Key Indicator of Wellness.*

Weisman, Avery D. 1984. *Coping Capacity: On the Nature of Being Mortal.* New York: Human Sciences Press.

Whitbourne, Susan Krauss. 1985. "The Psychological Construction of the Life Span." *Handbook of the Psychology of Aging.* Eds. James E. Birren and K. Warner Schaie. New York: Van Nostrand Reinhold, 594–618.

Willing, Jules Z. 1981. *The Reality of Retirement: The Inner Experience of Becoming a Retired Person.* New York: Morrow.

Wu, Zheng and Christoph M. Schimmele. 2007. "Uncoupling in Late Life." *Generations.* Vol. 31. No. 3. (Fall), 41–46.

Zaranek, Rochelle R. and Peter A. Lichtenberg. 2008. "Urban Elders and Casino Gambling: Are They at Risk of a Gambling Problem?" *Journal of Aging Studies.* Vol. 22. No. 1 (January), 13–23.

— ABOUT THE AUTHOR —

Upon obtaining an undergraduate degree in Nutrition/Business from Trinity University in San Antonio, Texas, Ruth Garrett began her rewarding journey through the world of higher education and lifelong learning.

Responding to her young son's desire to communicate with his Latino playmates, Garrett began taking private Spanish lessons with her son. She was able to polish these language skills while studying at the Universidad de Valencia, Catedra Mediterraneo—through Georgia University's Studies Abroad Program.

An opportunity to live in Europe, accompanying her flight surgeon spouse to assignment in Germany, led to the study of the German language and culture. While in Germany, Garrett attended the Friedrich-Alexander University of Nürnberg, once again with Georgia University's Studies Abroad Program.

Even with the ending of her first marriage, Ruth continued moving forward. In 1972, she completed her first master's degree, in education, at Georgia Southern University.

Her second marriage at the age of forty-two took her back to Germany, where she completed intensive courses at the Goethe-Institut in Munich and Ludwig-Maximilians-Universität München, eventually earning her PhD. The International

Education Evaluators (IEE) equated her degree into three doctorates in America: gerontology, German, and psychology.

At age sixty-three, Garrett completed her Master of Public Health degree, while teaching gerontology at two universities in Georgia. She also developed computer programs in Georgia and Tokyo with the telecommunications industries of Japan.

Garrett continued her international involvement in aging with presentations to the European Federation on Aging in Prague and the University of Poland at Gdansk. Nationally, she has presented aging issues in several states, on television, and for many civic and church groups.

Retiring from the University of Georgia educational system, a presentation at the Millennium Maxwell House Hotel led to an offer from the only geriatric education center in Tennessee (at that time housed at the old Meharry Medical College). A two-million-dollar grant funded the consortium (Meharry, Vanderbilt, and TSU), providing training to sixteen thousand health professionals for five years. Developing a Geriatric Certificate Program, implementing a course for medical students in aging issues, and founding a Geriatric Student Forum led to additional grant funding that continued her work for three more years.

Changing speed but not focus, Garrett is currently a consultant to universities, hospitals, and colleges in Georgia,

Tennessee, and Kentucky. The development of local Community without Walls programs—designed to keep seniors Aging in Place, while actively swimming, dancing, and gardening, as well as taking Spanish college courses—continue to keep her mentally and physically active. This energetic and creative septuagenarian practices what she preaches because as Robert Frost poetically stated, "We have miles to go before we sleep."